The Guards Spoke Russian

The Guards Spoke Russian
Memoir of a Ukrainian Jew in a Soviet Gulag

ARYEH MALKISH

Foreword by Alexander Kazarnovsky

McFarland & Company, Inc., Publishers
Jefferson, North Carolina

Previous editions of this book have been published in Ukrainian as *Московщина* (*Moscowity*) by the Ukrainian Publishing Association, London (1978); in Russian under the same title by Moria (1984); in Hebrew as גרוח קרא לש הנורכיז (*Memories from a Stepmother Land*) by Sunny Sale (1998); and in English as *Memories from a Stepmother Land: Exposing the Roots of the Conflict in Ukraine* by Contento de Semrik (2014). Translation by Joan Talkowsky.

All illustrations were created by Victor Boguslavsky.

LIBRARY OF CONGRESS CATALOGUING-IN-PUBLICATION DATA

Names: Malkish, Aryeh, 1947– author.
Title: The guards spoke Russian : memoir of a Ukrainian Jew in a Soviet gulag / Aryeh Malkish ; foreword by Alexander Kazarnovsky.
Other titles: Moscowity. English
Description: Jefferson, North Carolina : McFarland & Company, Inc., 2023 | "Previous editions of this book have been published in Ukrainian as Московщина (Moscowity) by the Ukrainian Publishing Association, London (1978); in Russian under the same title by Moria (1984); in Hebrew as זיכרונה של ארץ חורג (Memories from a Stepmother Land) by Sunny Sale (1998); and in English as Memories from a Stepmother Land: Exposing the Roots of the Conflict in Ukraine by Contento de Semrik (2014). Translation by Joan Talkowsky"—Title page verso.
Identifiers: LCCN 2023004795 | ISBN 9781476691510 (paperback : acid free paper) ∞
ISBN 9781476649443 (ebook)
Subjects: LCSH: Malkish, Aryeh, 1947– | Political prisoners—Soviet Union—Biography. | Jews—Soviet Union—Biography.
Classification: LCC HV8959.R9 M27713 2023 | DDC 365/.45092 [B]—dc23/eng/20230221
LC record available at https://lccn.loc.gov/2023004795

BRITISH LIBRARY CATALOGUING DATA ARE AVAILABLE

ISBN (print) 978-1-4766-9151-0
ISBN (ebook) 978-1-4766-4944-3

© 2023 Aryeh Malkish. All rights reserved

No part of this book may be reproduced or transmitted in any form or by any means, electronic or mechanical, including photocopying or recording, or by any information storage and retrieval system, without permission in writing from the publisher.

On the cover: old observation tower in abandoned Soviet Gulag (Vladimir Mulder/Shutterstock)

Printed in the United States of America

McFarland & Company, Inc., Publishers
Box 611, Jefferson, North Carolina 28640
www.mcfarlandpub.com

Table of Contents

*Foreword: Of Past and Future
   by Alexander Kazarnovsky*   1

Preface   5

Change of destination   7

Hidden light   10

A day in the cell   14

Domovoy (the poltergeist)   19

Rest   20

Toes the line   20

The camp   23

A Brahmin in solitary   25

Jews in the camp   32

The operating methods of the KGB   34

Prisoners' pathologies   36

Corruption   41

The liberators are coming!   43

Divide and rule   49

The slave mentality   52

The surprise   53

The Jewish "conspiracy"   56

Nixon to you!   60

Table of Contents

A new man	61
The big transfer from Mordovia to the Urals	63
The ship of fools	71
Back to the wire	76
Minus 54° Centigrade	78
The kidnapped spring	82
A white cockroach	84
Two months in solitary	89
The usual way	93
The cell is flooded	99
Triangle	105
Criminal-political	107
A Chinese meal	108
News of the imprisonment	109
"I'd like to die"	111
Working flesh	116
The monastery of silence	117
Jacob and the cannibal	118
The dam burst	125
The whirlpool of terror	133
Gog and Magog	137
A violent departure	141
The Urals again	146
Toward the exodus	153
Index	154

Symbol of Communist Russia.

Foreword: Of Past and Future

by Alexander Kazarnovsky

I spent 42 years in the Soviet Union. (I cannot say I lived there because dwelling there cannot be called "life.") But only after reading Arie Malkish's memoirs which had been published in Israel in 1984 did I realize the depth of the abyss we had been in.

As for the present moment, the book really looks prophetic—A. Malkish has shown the source and the root of the nightmare which is taking place in Ukraine nowadays.

However I should say he was lucky. After he had created a dissident organization in which 300 people from 16 cities participated, he was sentenced to seven years in prisons and concentration camps. But the environment he spent those seven years in proved to become the shell out of which the new Russia would hatch years afterwards.

Malkish shows that the teenagers' mentality in the USSR was greatly affected by criminal "romance." Criminal behavior became an ideal for the youth in post–Soviet Russia. Here one can find the reason behind Russian atrocities in Bucha, Irpen, etc.

On the other hand, a criminal must be an adversary to any kind of authority. He is free of any loyalty... Not in Russia! Malkish writes, "A Russian man can stay in prison for twenty years and after that, take a machine-gun and fight to defend his 'happy' life!"

"Who slaughtered the Hungarians in 1848? Who abused Poland? Who drowned the Chinese as if they were puppies in the river during the Russo-Japanese War? Who enslaved Latvia, the Caucasus, the Ukraine, and a hundred or two hundred other peoples throughout hundreds of years? Who profited from all that? Who were the only ones in the 20th century to retain a colonial empire? Who increased their population, not by births, but by conquering other peoples? And who, in spite of this, had lost a considerable part of its people inside barbed wire fences or through organized starvation? Who is standing on the brink of national death?"

Mind you, these lines were not written by A. Malkish today, not even in 2014! They were written 42 years ago! What has changed since then? Nothing!

Here is one more quotation: "This was no life. It would have been preferable to flee to the forest. Every night there were new explosions, fires, robberies, murders, rapes. The soldiers even raped murdered women, and raped children."

Is this a reference to Russian soldiers in present-day Ukraine? No, it is about Russians in postwar Lithuania.

Another interesting thing we learn from this book is that in the camp there were two groups of Ukrainians—so called *polizei*s, those who had collaborated with Germans during World War II and former militants of the OUN and the UPA—e.g., Ukrainian partisan armies which had fought both against Germans and Russians for the national independence of Ukraine. While the *polizei*s showed open hatred towards Jews, the militants of the OUN and the UPA so-called *banderovtsi* whom modern Russian propaganda accuses of Nazism—were quite sympathetic.

"One of the most surprising things in the political camps," writes A. Malkish, "was the friendly treatment accorded the Zionists by the members of the Ukrainian nationalists."

At times, it was of great, decisive importance. Because the Ukrainians made up nearly half of the political prisoners, their influence was also great with the other nationalist communities, imprisoned like them because of their opposition to the Russian occupation. This wasn't only lip service, but active identification and participation in protests for mutual defense in the face of persecution.

In Camp 35 in the Urals, in the Perm district, when the criminal element incited by the KGB tried to organize a pogrom against the Zionist community, the Ukrainians stopped them and threatened:

Foreword: Of Past and Future

"If you touch the Jews, you'll have us to deal with!" The rioters were frightened. They had good reason to flinch. The veteran partisans, who had fought Hitler and Stalin, weren't just bandying words.

The Ukrainian political prisoners—both the partisans as well as the young, educated ones—were mostly positive and pleasant, very far from the common stereotype....

And—perhaps most important for understanding the current reasons of the war in Ukraine are the following facts given in this book: "The quantitative ratio between Russians to Ukrainians in the Soviet empire at the beginning of the Revolution was 1.5:1 and now it stood at 3:1. Approximately 11 million Russians flooded the Ukraine, which had been emptied of nearly half of its original inhabitants through starvation, collectivization, and the mass purges. Most of those remaining feared opening their mouths in their mother tongue. There are those who have said that even at the time these lines were written, most of the white population of Siberia and the Caucasus consisted of Ukrainian exiles and their offspring."

Reading this book, one realizes that the present-day bloodshed in Ukraine has been being prepared by Russia over tens if not hundreds of years.

But now, as we see, the war in Ukraine is moving towards its end. The Russian army is suffering defeat after defeat. Why so? Why is there the lack of arms, ammunition, fuel for tanks? Why are Russian soldiers constantly hungry? Where have trillions of dollars, which the largest country in the world has spent on its army, gone?

The answers to these questions we can also find in this book.

It is fitting here to note that in Soviet Russia, theft and disappearances were a matter of routine. In shops or slaughterhouses, dining rooms and restaurants, this was figured into the worker's stipulated salary. "If you don't steal—you won't live." This history of theft, bribery, and corruption had been going on in an uninterrupted chain since the days of "Ivan the Terrible."

And now let us see how a modern Russian journalist, Yulia Latynina, has commented on the situation: "The Ukrainian army was gathered for the war by means of SMSes; the Russian one by means of orders to the army. Ukrainian volunteers brought food, technique and drones. Russian conscripts stole all such things."

So my friends, read this book—it is not only about the past. It is also about the future.

Alexander Kazarnovsky is an Israeli writer, a laureate of "The Olive of Jerusalem Prize," Aldanov competition Prize, Grand Prix at the International Literature competition named by Sasha Cherny, Akmatov Prize for Small Proze, Hertfordshire Press Award "Bestseller" (2022).

Preface

When I was spending week after week alone in an icy starving dungeon or in a prison cell full of hungry cockroaches ready to attack you the moment you go to sleep, the only thought that saved me was that one day I would tell the world the truth about Russia. And indeed those who read it told me afterwards that it had opened their eyes more than any other book.

There in Gulag I clearly realized that their empire is the embodiment of the word *evil*.

What is new in that book? It is the characterization of relations between Russia and the nations it had enslaved, and especially this applies to Ukraine.

In secret cellars and concentration camps created by Cheka their ideal unattainable utopia just at a moment's notice turned into a murderous anti-utopia.

The next phase of illusions was so called anti–Nazism, though it was Stalin who raised Hitler to power, it was Stalin who forged a fraternal alliance with him, and captured Europe together with him. And then both bandits started to fight dividing the prey.

After 30 years of kleptocracy the barbarous war against Ukraine and the revival of *idée-fixe* of Russian world domination at all costs. Modern Russian folk poetry is also unique in the world:

> "This land's not your land
> It's only my land
> From Middle Asia
> To the New York Island
> And our power
> Will never end
> The world will become a Russian land!"

That is my motivation for this present publication.

Change of destination

On July 30, 1969, I was packing my old suitcases with a light heart. My documents were ready, and my ticket sat in my pocket for the first train leaving Ryazan for western Ukraine where there was some chance to obtain a visa for Israel. My brother and I had no room in the student dorms at the Technical University for Electronic Engineering in Ryazan. We had been forced to rent a corner in a private apartment in crammed quarters which can hardly be described.

My last "apartment" was on a tree-lined street, not far from the institute where I studied. The landlady was an energetic, red-cheeked grandmother, who wore old-fashioned, round-framed eyeglasses, and knew how to make money. However, my brother and I got along with her. Her husband, an old, yellow-mustached, blue-eyed amputee and drunkard, red and bleary-eyed, used to chase her with an axe in his hand and demand money from her, so that he could relieve the pains of drunkenness.

The old woman used to run outdoors screaming, or hide in our small room. Her husband also used to ask us for a three-note (three rubles, the price of a bottle), but without the threat of his axe. The old lady had a 90-year-old mother, bed-ridden and in a constant state of confusion, whom she used to beat brutally while screaming "Drop dead already! Drop dead already!" When her mother finally obeyed her request, she gave her a resplendent funeral with a requiem mass, commemorative repast, etc.

The landlady was religious. Her house was full of icons and old prayer books. Occasionally, other women of her age would come to visit, her sisters in faith. She sometimes presented us with deep theological questions: "Who is your God? Isn't it Pilate?"

The Guards Spoke Russian

Hearing our explanation, she'd nod her grey head with its symmetrical part under her kerchief, attributing great importance to our words, but it seemed that she didn't understand a thing. In the future, when she was called to testify, she didn't testify against us.

My brother and I slept in the same bed, but the old woman thought it didn't take enough advantage of the space. Therefore, she placed another folding bed in the room for another tenant. He too was a student, the son of a Russian colonel from Ukraine. He used to drink unceasingly with his friends, drunk ruffians like himself. Within days he would use up the entire amount of the monthly scholarship he received, as well as his financial assistance from home. He would then ask us for handouts or for at least enough to buy black bread. That and more. Due to the cold, he and his friends would bring loose women to our room. Because of these never-ending orgies, we were often afraid to go home.

The odor emanating from our roommate was intolerable. Dirt didn't prevent him from dressing up in a shirt as white as snow, which he sprayed with eau de cologne. After he had finally been expelled from the institute and drafted into the army, not before filling our bed with wine, we were able to breathe again. We offered the landlady higher rent, just so she wouldn't add a third tenant again.

Thus, it would be easy to understand how I parted from the domestic warmth which looked down on me from the faded green, wooden walls of my room, while sitting on my packed suitcase. On that very day my brother was already at our parents' home in eastern Ukraine.

Suddenly a knock was heard at the door.

"We're from the KGB," the meaty men wearing brimmed hats presented themselves as they entered the room. "Here is a search warrant!"

For some reason, I felt complete calm, the calm of death. While they confiscated typescripts of Jabotinsky's articles, a novel by Bulgakov and something else, I destroyed a note which contained addresses and telephone numbers without them sensing it. They didn't confiscate the Soviet books in Yiddish with which I had tried to learn the language, or even "A Thousand Words" (Part One), but only leafed through them. Afterward, they drove me in the Volga automobile of the secret police to the KGB's drab building. The background to the arrest was our student home meetings in which we'd discussed ideological issues not to the regime's liking.

Colonel Markelov, with a dark and swollen face, sat in his spacious office. He tried to instill me with fear and demanded that I tell him everything about myself including my relationship with the "Zionist International" (as he called it). I responded that I didn't have to answer his questions.

"Don't you understand where you are?" Markelov asked me with emphasis, as he stared into my eyes. I answered that in the civilized world, organizations such as his only deal with catching spies.

"And aren't you a spy?" the colonel asked tensely, tilting his body toward me.

"Not yet," I answered with a dismal grin.

"Nonetheless, it will yet be proven that we don't only deal with such matters," Markelov answered, and indicated his underlings with his head. They moved me to another, even smaller room. There the investigations unit commander sat, Major Skonikov, also dressed in civilian clothing. His appearance was that of a storybook troll, gaunt, cynical, his stare that of a boa constrictor. He began to enumerate sporadic statistics about the activities of our home meetings in order to create the impression that he and his friends already knew everything. However, they didn't know everything. Skonikov mixed up different issues and didn't understand the connections between things. As my comrades and I had agreed in advance, I refused "to assist" him. He pushed a piece of paper toward me and demanded that I write down a list of my acquaintances.

"No," I answered determinedly.

Skonikov placed an arrest warrant in front of me and proceeded to fill out the protocol.

"Why do you refuse to provide testimony?" he shouted and slammed his fist on the table.

"I refuse to explain the reason."

"We'll put you in a psychiatric institution! For observation...," he added with a malicious smile.

The Guards Spoke Russian

His threats did not avail, and the same Volga automobile that had brought me there took me to the old city jail, built in the Queen Catherine style. I was shoved into a small, box-like room and the door slammed shut behind me.

This was a narrow, long room. It had a bench, a can for bodily functions, and a light bulb. There was no room to move around. There was a peephole in the door, with its cover on the outside, and from time to time, it swayed.

The search in my room and the investigation had lasted half a day and I was already very tired and hungry. I sat down on the edge of the bench, lay down on my back with my hands crossed across my chest and my feet jammed into the floor because the bench was too short. My back nearly broke as a result.

After some time, the lock creaked. I opened my eyes and stood up. They took me out of the cell, removed my clothes and did a detailed body search. At the end of the search, they wrote a report, ordered me to get dressed and led me to the bathhouse next to a high fence surrounding the prison yard. The fence was draped with barbed wire and an alarm. It had a watchtower and a strip of plowed land next to it. They shaved my head in the bathhouse.

Only when I felt the strands of my hair falling upon my knees did I realize that my previous life had come to an end. Now a new chapter was beginning. They led me to the prison steps, through the corridors, accompanied by guards whose hands held a bunch of rattling keys. They opened the door to one of the cells. Inside I saw the repulsive faces of the criminals. Someone offered me bread the consistency of clay. They assigned me a filthy mattress and blanket. I could rest.

Hidden light

Before entering solitary, the prisoner's clothes are removed. His clothes and shoes are taken away and he is left wearing only an undershirt and underpants. For an outer garment, he receives a light cotton coverall, not necessarily clean, generally torn, worn, and lacking buttons. His prisoner's cap is also taken away. He is left with special wood-sole sandals for solitary. When he leaves solitary, those items are left for his heir. The solitary confinement cell is best described as follows: a small, concrete, subterranean coffin. The walls are covered with splashes of concrete called a "robe."

It creates a frightening impression. Grey dust, accumulated over years, covers the rough wall. Solitary confinement is in the basement. It has a small, elevated window covered with many thick, iron bars, and opaque glass which makes the cell dim. The door is padded with a layer of perforated iron, like a hive. Drilled from the cell's exterior to its interior, the sharp edges from the drilled perforations don't allow for banging on the door—the remnants of the drilling might cause bloody wounds. Above the door, a brick protrudes from the wall. The opening this forms is barred. Inside this opening a weak incandescent lamp is placed which lights the cell with an orange light, casting interweaving shadows of the bars on the ceiling. A marble stool is set in the wall with barely enough room for a child's hip, so that it can't be used for sitting for a long time.

The table is a bit larger and made of stone. It is cold, so that it's unpleasant to lie upon. The floor is made of freezing-cold cement. No lying upon it, no sitting on it. There is filth everywhere. There is no wash basin. The slop bucket can be found by its odor before it's seen in the ever-growing gloom. The atmosphere is damp, compressed, and full of moisture. And cold. Mostly inescapable cold. There is nothing to cover oneself with. There's nothing to do in solitary, nothing to read, no one to talk to. No information of any kind comes in. The prisoner lives in an absolute vacuum. Once every two days a warm, liquid mixture is given to the prisoner.

During the "flight" days in Soviet solitary confinement—the odd-numbered days—no hot food is given. The prisoner's only nourishment is water and 450 grams of damp, black bread.

During the night the prisoner is given a "helicopter"—a board made of planks roughly joined together, which the guard throws on the cold floor. It's generally colder down there, adding further to the suffering of already frozen feet.

Dungeon

    At ten at night the board is brought in. It is taken out of the cell at six in the morning. The caloric value of the food is lower than what is required to maintain the body's minimal energy output even under the best conditions of rest.

Hidden light

A person can adapt to any situation, can get used to anything. However, the first experience of these compounded tortures is unbearable. Until my imprisonment, I had become used to a full, strenuous rhythm of life. Now, suddenly there was total, endless, distressing emptiness. I was particularly bothered by the thought that this was only the beginning. From now on, this horror would only increase and would crush me to death. So why, then, put off the end?

While feeling around, I found an old piece of lard on the cold radiator. It was unclear how it had gotten there, and its stench overwhelmed me. Was it there only by chance? In a tiny depression in the dust-filled wall under the radiator, an aluminum spoon handle had been forgotten, a metal implement. It could be useful...

An unusual event saved me from thinking about death. It was the most mysterious and the most intense event in my life. It happened while I was dozing in an uncomfortable, twisted position on the stone stool, depleted of strength by walking long hours from one corner to the other in my concrete grave. I didn't know whether or not I was sleeping, nor did I know how much time had passed (watches were removed before entering). When I lifted my head, the opaque window was painted with evening's deep purple. The checkered lighting formed by the ray of light on the ceiling through the bars stood out still more. The chequers of shadow were trapezoidal, narrow on the bottom and widening toward the top. Everything was in its place, while at the same time, changed beyond recognition.

The cell was as if transparent; the splendor of an exalted happiness washed over me. The grave of suffering trembled with non-human happiness, and was full of overflowing joy. I fell on the floor in a warm prayer, combining words in Hebrew and Russian. This was a prayer of thanksgiving. I felt everything very tangibly, with lucid consciousness. I understood that never in my life had I known, nor apparently would I know, anything that approached this experience of pure, holy, impossible happiness. This was a blowing of the eternal in which all evil disappeared without leaving a trace. Everything external, superficial and secondary disappeared. This wasn't an internal flame, similar to the gloomy flame in a black cave. Rather, it was a quiet eternal flame. This sense of presence slowly and gradually left me, gradually weakening day by day. It cooled off without haste, like the sea, but left me with an unforgettable memory.

I will never forget how I fell asleep on the bare planks with an intense, joyful smile. Neither cold nor pain, neither evil nor death, existed for me. Not only did I have no need for anything, but on the contrary, I didn't know upon whom or how to bestow the joy that completely filled me. Only several days later, when only a portion of that experience remained, did I remember my hunger and how tasty the thin mixture of coarse groats had been! To this day, I remember how my eyes lit up when I ate (I felt it so acutely), and how every cell in my body had been filled. In situations like this, it is impossible to astound, to shock, to enchant the ordinary person. It is the newness of the experience that leaves the most intense impression.

With the completion of my period of punishment in solitary, I was removed as I was and brought to the interrogation room. Skonikov and Chetin sat with reports in front of them, expecting to see a broken, subservient individual. Easy prey. Instead, they saw a happy, pale, shaven-headed prisoner, dressed in his odd coverall, freely declaring that now he had nothing to discuss with them, that solitary had been a means of exerting pressure on him, and now he did not intend to sign any document. As was customary, they lied and said that this was the first time they had heard about solitary confinement and that my being there didn't depend upon them. I brazenly giggled, standing silently until I was led back to my cell.

A day in the cell

The buzz of waking up. The night bulb now extinguished; the day bulb coming on. Prisoners, now awake, begin to move about. It was a happy time in my new cell.

The dominant prisoner in the cell was a fair-haired thug whose strength was inexhaustible. It turned out that he wasn't quite balanced. He was the "rat," the cell's informer. His sly, narrow, grey eyes were always gleaming in his wide-jawed, slightly tanned face. The other prisoners were passive.

The thug beneath me in the bunk bed quickly dressed in his filthy prisoner's coat over his underwear. With an idiotic smile, he stuck his dirty feet into my shoes, crushing them in the back (he threw his boots to the side). He ran to the heating pipe descending from the radiator, while holding an aluminum cup missing its handle. He hit the pipe a number of pre-arranged times, placed the bottom of the cup against the pipe's metal and shouted into it: "Girls, girls, g…o…o…d morning!" A rapping reply came from down below.

The thug reversed the cup with its opening to the pipe and placed his ear against the bottom of the cup. We heard a typical metallic sound, like that of speaking into a defective phone. With his ear to the cup, however, he clearly heard the returned greetings. As well as transmitted questions such as "How did you sleep?" with their replies, we were also subjected to coarse stories about the night's dreams, promises of love, and other such nonsense. Suddenly the food window silently opened. The guard gave a significant look to the thug who was too engaged in conversation with his beloved Galka to notice what was occurring around him, despite the prohibition against any contact between cells. They spoke in detail into each other's ears of what they would do if they by chance happened to be in one cell … and finally after he had properly enjoyed the conversation, the guard with a thick voice cut off the lovers' conversation, like a cat enjoying his trapped mouse: "Will you be discussing things much longer?"

The thug, startled, immediately turned around, rapped twice on the pipe to signal "disperse" and ran to the window. "'Nachalnichek' (a fawning term of endearment for someone in charge), I won't do it again, I promise, this was the last time. My beloved is there. Don't write up a report, okay?" The words shot out of his mouth like out of a machine gun.

"Beloved," smiled the guard, satisfied. "What do you know? Maybe this beloved is eighty years old?"

"Really, the lying bitch, she says she's twenty-seven! I'll show her, Nachalnichek! And now, let me go to the bathroom for a bowl of water to wash the floor with!"

The Guards Spoke Russian

"Yes, you're on duty today," the guard smiled.

The thug pretended that he was absorbed in washing the floor, but essentially he poured water between the cracks so that water would begin to drip from the ceiling in the girls' cell below. Tapping on the pipe from below was soon heard, and afterward, through the window, came an intense stream of swearing. At that moment, the small window opened and food was sent in. Fat Mashke, a prisoner, passed by in her white coat with a grey soup ladle, and distributed food to each prisoner in his aluminum bowl.

When the prisoners held out their bowls to the window, they tried to pinch her affectionately. She'd been carrying on a romance with one of them for some time. At every opportunity, they imagined their future life together aloud or by note. When the guard wasn't looking, the prisoner even managed to place his hand on her bosom. In addition to this small pleasure, he also got thicker goo into his bowl. We waded in the puddles of water on the floor and sat down on the rough wooden benches around the table.

After breakfast, the bowls were taken from us. Suddenly, the person responsible for our section arrived and demanded to stop flooding the cell beneath us.

"Who are we flooding?" the thug impertinently wondered.

"You, ice-eyed bastard, I would show you a thing or two!" and the person in charge left growling.

The criminal prisoners sat down to play dominoes. They smoked Mahorka, a coarse Russian tobacco. The smokers used to roll it in newspaper and smoke. Their homemade cigarettes were very strong. I went up on the top bunk with a book by Tolstoy or Dostoyevsky, and despite the satanic tumult of the noisy radio and the shouts from below, I disengaged and submerged into the world of literature.

The noise of the dominoes was deafening, the smoke stung my eyes, and the cell was filled with meaningless shouting.

"Comrades, they're taking the chicks for a walk!" Someone stopped the game, hearing the banging of keys on the door of the cell below us (that's how they informed the prisoners to get ready for a walk). I was often impressed by the ability of the criminals to re-create an actual picture of what went on in the prison according to

A day in the cell

slight hints. The thug mixed up the dominoes and took a small stick with a small mirror attached to it out from under the slop bucket. While standing like an acrobat on the window, he tried to see the path which led to the exercise yard and the "chicks" who were being led there under our window with the use of his "periscope." All of this was accompanied by moans of desire and lascivious descriptions.

"That's it, they're waving hello!" shouted the thug. "Help me write a 'lesser'!"* Laughing crazily and talking loudly, his cellmates helped him with his note, and the usual subject dominated: Oh, if we could only break a hole in the floor, then...

"We need to make a 'horse'!" the thug shouted again. A "horse" was a rope, by means of which notes or small packages were lowered to the cells below.

The criminals tore a mattress covering, a grey, cotton sack in which the prisoners slept, and cut narrow strips from it. Idiotic, primitive, wild melodies at a deafening volume were emitted by the radio. I was shuddering all over as the criminals were dancing happily and stamping their feet.

The women were brought back from their walk. The thug again fell on the pipe, persuading, promising Mahorka, asking to make up and demanding that they take the "horse" from him. To pass the rope with its cargo through the narrow space between the iron slats, and to lower it so that they could grab it from the window beneath us, required real artistry. There are even several virtuosos who had managed to pass the "horse" sideways, on the diagonal. They fastened the rope on a hook at the window below, brought it into the cell, took the "mail" and pulled on the rope to signal that it could be raised back up.

All that time, someone stood next to the door covering the eyehole. Suddenly, the food window opened with a loud noise. The acrobat somersaulted from the window. Apparently, Mashke had brought lunch and the guard wasn't quick enough to discover anything. Sometimes the guards discovered the "horse" from outside down

---

*"Lesser" = "letter" in the Ashkenazic pronunciation, which the Russian criminals somehow had grasped and used in their secret language so that the police wouldn't understand.

below. They would grab it and tear the cargo off the rope, bringing their catch to the office of the deputy of operations.

After lunch, the deafening rattle of the big key in the iron door could be heard. Now we were being called out for a walk.

I tried as much as possible to look at the sky through the screen of bars above the exercise enclosure. The eyes could rest and it was generally pleasant. Because of the long hours in the dim cell, the sky appeared to have bold colors and great depth, highlighted by cirrus clouds.

The thug began to harass me, to threaten me, to hurl epithets and nicknames at me and said that I was so and so, that he had served at the border defending me like a patrol dog. "Who did you guard me from?" I asked wondering. He continued to grumble, but didn't dare start a quarrel or hadn't received the appropriate orders to do it.

After the walk, everyone lay down to sleep. The cell looked even dimmer and darker after our eyes had gotten used to the clear sunlight.

In the evening, the thug tended to have "clarity of mind," but there was no vodka and what could be had in its place? How to "tie one on"? Finally he took heart and undertook a dangerous experiment. He soaked Mahorka in a cup of water and drank the concentrate. Soon, his face turned green. He grabbed his stomach, bent over the slop bucket and vomited. After he had recovered a bit, he barely toddled over to his bed, turned his head away and said, "I really tied one on! I saw three cells at once. What a blast!"

With the signal of the lights-out bell, women's shouting was heard through the windows: "Boys, g…o…o…d night!" accompanied by laughter, coarseness, and swearing.

From a cell somewhere a barking dog could be heard (whoever lost at dominoes had to bark out the window the number of times equal to the number of points he had lost in the game).

From another cell came the clear voice of an invisible youth: "Prison, prison, give me nickname!" Among the criminals it was accepted to give each other nicknames and not to use our given names. A new prisoner had to be given a nickname so that he could be like everyone else.

"What are you in for?" asked a deep bass voice.
"Rape!" chirped the minor.
"Midwife!" the bass voice bestowed him with the nickname he had chosen.
"Thanks, prison!"

Domovoy (the poltergeist)

Sometimes there were nice guys among the criminals.

One of them was a dark, tall, and solid guy, almost totally bald, merry and sociable. This wasn't his first prison term. Once he had stolen something and another time, he had carried on when drunk. Immediately, he pronounced judgment upon the thug who was with us: "Informer. You can smell those wolves a mile away."

I liked to listen to his stories. He told them without excessive swearing, although his language was picturesque and juicy. An interesting subject that came up in his stories was that of a domovoy (poltergeist) and his encounters with it. According to him, the domovoy was an invisible, hairy creature, connected to a particular dwelling and the family who lived there. It was mischievous, but was not considered to be a negative force. In Russia, this folklore was stronger than Christianity. The domovoy had visited the bald man for the first time while he was still a child. While he was lying on the stove, suddenly an invisible, hairy body touched his body. He screamed, but his mother calmed him down: "That's the poltergeist, one of ours, and you don't need to be afraid of it. It's making your acquaintance. Next time, ask it what it's come to tell us, whether something good or bad."

After many years passed and he was sitting in prison for the first time, the bald man woke up one morning and felt that something was pressing against him, not letting him breathe…

"What did you come to tell me?" the prisoner remembered to whisper.

"A good sign!" the poltergeist replied and let him be. And indeed, after a short time, the bald man was released early.

Rest

Except for critical moments during interrogation, I must admit that I never experienced such complete rest and absolute calm as I did in prison. You no longer felt detached. You knew that you had landed on the firm ground, and mainly, you had no worries. Nothing depended on you. Everything was over. Apparently, rest like this was only to be found in the afterlife.

Prison indeed was reminiscent of life after death. Every person fears thinking about prison just like he fears thinking about death. However, the latter cannot be escaped. "Free" citizens (those who hadn't yet been arrested) became cross-eyed feeling fear and danger of the short-haired "ghosts," the prisoners who sometimes appeared in train stations, being transported from one place to another, unclear from where and unclear how. Then the knowledge would creep into the consciousness of those living ones that in their midst there existed an isolated and invisible world of the living dead: a kingdom of shades that lived according to special rules. Only rarely did it overlap the world of living people involved in it. However, there was only a slight chance that one of the living would know that these dead, imprisoned through no fault of their own, could exist there, in the life beyond, with the pleasure of inconceivable and unknowable calm.

Toes the line

Sometimes the criminal prisoners spoke about courts, laws, prosecutors and other current events. Malishev, one of the prisoners, complained about the prosecutor's speech demanding to deny the accused freedom and the judge who pronounced sentence "in the name of the Russian Federal Republic!"

Malishev distorted the words a bit and from his mouth it sounded like "the Russian Pederastic Republic," but that subject quickly lost interest. The criminals started to argue about the "fork" structure of some motorcycle; I was absorbed in a book and didn't pay attention to the emotions heating up as time went on. Finally, I disengaged from the book. The shouting had become already too great and it was impossible to concentrate. What had happened? Hadn't they become tired of that "fork" yet? Matters had taken a negative turn. Offensive threats were coming from Malishev's direction. Zanosov, who was weaker, stood up and with a plaintive tone said: "So, come at me!"

I managed to separate them just in time, because the furious, red-eyed Malishev already held a spoon with a sharpened handle used to cut bread. I barely separated them and calmed them down. What had gone on? Why hadn't they gotten along? Did their life depend on this "fork?"

After this incident, Zanosov began to respect me and told me about his life. Malishev had already fallen asleep and was snoring heavily. We sat on Zanosov's bed and spoke about what had brought him here.

Zanosov was a simple lad. A worker. His drunkard father had spent all the family's assets on drink. He had been a coarse, rude man who abused and beat his wife. When Zanosov grew up, he began giving it back to his father in order to protect his mother. What remained besides work and home? Drinking friends, and women. When the guys got together in the evening, they couldn't refrain from drinking. After they had drunk enough, all stops were pulled out. Marriage also hadn't saved him from the mire. He was bored in his wife's company! He mostly went out with his friends who were married as well. After some "binge" with his group, he wound up in a storeroom with a prostitute. After a short time, he discovered that he had become infected with gonorrhea. Disgusting. And shameful for him with his wife! No matter. He was cured and his wife forgave him. Everything was okay … and just then, he was accused of participating in a gang rape. Now, he was here with no way out. His wife was pregnant and was soon to give birth ... how would he be able to meet her gaze at the trial?

It was strange that the most likeable and least damaged of the criminals that I had encountered was sitting in jail, accused of participating in the gang rape of a minor.

Only after I had sat for a long time with Zanosov in the same cell, did I begin to understand what had brought him to such a low point. He wasn't a bad guy. It was just that in the company of others he completely lost a will of his own. I imagined that his companions were no different. I suppose that none of them separately would have done such a thing. Certainly not Zanosov. But together they had become a collective beast, lacking judgment and inhibition. When they were in a group, not one of them thought about personal responsibility. Not one of them asked himself "What am I doing?" If only one of them had uttered those words, the others would have sobered up and stopped. However, the behavior of the group as a whole was much lower than that of each of its members. Although the "Malishevs" in the society were a minority, unfortunately, the society itself became one big "Malishev...."

I read the prosecution's summation submitted against Zanosov. The summation consisted of the rape victim's testimony. In Zanosov's opinion, she had tried to clear herself and therefore, hadn't referred to some important facts. Zanosov didn't have any reason to deceive me as he described the chain of events. One evening, three of the guys met, all of them young, married, one already a father, the wife of another about to give birth. As was customary, they got drunk and went looking for action. They left the place and saw two girls. They didn't even have the clear view of them. One of the guys, who was more daring, approached to "arrange things." Seeing that they were drunk, one of the girls quickly ran off. The other one was curious as well and she also wanted to spite some boy in her class.

After one of the drunks and the girl had reached an agreement, he invited his friends to join them.

Zanosov and his other friend purposely lagged behind and kept their distance, so as not to disturb. They walked slowly, in the darkness, through the field by the town. Suddenly Zanosov bumped into a bush and in the dim light of the moon, he saw the couple lying beneath it. His arrogant friend had nearly finished disrobing the "lady" and she seemed not dissatisfied. Zanosov felt intimidated and went to stand aside with his other friend. They had already moved off quite a distance when they heard a shout. When they turned their heads, they saw a naked girl fleeing from their rude friend.

"Catch her!" he yelled. That shout was enough to turn them into one irresponsible, predatory beast. Zanosov and his friend thoughtlessly ran toward the girl, like hounds who had heard the call to the chase. It seemed that at the very last moment, the girl had been reluctant to lose her virginity, had broken away from the thug and had started to run away. She had been too late. The wild gang overtook her next to the cornfield and knocked her to the ground. One of them tore off a large ear of corn and threatened to beat her with it if she resisted. Then something shameful occurred: due to the drunkenness, the chase, or their over-enthusiasm, none of the three had the strength to perform. One of them had the idea of manually arousing himself and the others followed his example. The three had been full partners in the deed. Afterward, they all went home. When the girl returned home late at night, she found her mother inflamed by the story she had heard from the girlfriend who had escaped at the beginning of events. She had heard that her daughter had gone off somewhere with a bunch of drunk, tough guys. After she heard the details from her daughter, she hastened to the police. The girlfriend who had fled remembered Zanosov's slanted eyelid. The police easily found the guilty ones who had already been under observation for some time. Only now, during the trial, did Zanosov look at his victim. According to him, the girl was ugly. He never would have wanted her. Here you have it! None of them was sentenced to death, but their prison terms were nearly the maximum.

The camp

Nearly a year after my arrest, in 1970, I was sentenced to seven years in prison and I was transferred to a camp with a harsh regime:

The Guards Spoke Russian

A barrack in the camp.

Camp 19 in Dovervlag in Mordovia, designated for "state prisoners," meaning "political prisoners."

The Russian gulag labor camp (or concentration camp), was a desolate square of territory, surrounded by fences, barbed wire, a strip of plowed land, guard towers, guard dogs, floodlights and special means for discovering someone in a forbidden zone. The square was divided in two with no free passage between the halves. One half had scattered, densely inhabited barracks, a headquarters and a dining room. Although only under duress could the concoction distributed in the camp be given the name "food." Cattle fodder—perhaps. The other half was designated for some kind of factory where the enslaved prisoners worked from morning to night. The camp also had punishment cells, solitary confinement.

However, that wasn't what particularly surprised me. I had already read underground literature about these institutions. It became clear to me that even here, censorship operated. This time, willingly. I am referring to the national composition of the political prisoners. I was surprised by the fact that Russians were a small minority in the camp. The Russian language was mainly heard spoken by the guards. Nearly half of the prisoners spoke Ukrainian. Most of the rest spoke Baltic languages, Armenian, etc.

As usual, a deep acquaintance with the place happened in solitary confinement which was also here.

A Brahmin in solitary

Slava Merkushev and Narkhov belonged to anti–Semitic groups and treated me with suspicion. However, solitary confinement did its job. Narkhov needed to express his natural dramatic talent, and Merkushev had to share his knowledge with someone, so gradually the atmosphere thawed.

Narkhov had been a deserter, a returning citizen. He had deserted from the occupying Soviet army from East Germany to West Germany.

The Guards Spoke Russian

He then returned and was arrested. Why had he returned? What had been lacking? Only one thing: the closed fist, the whip. A simple soldier like him got his salary in Germany and his eyes popped out. What, all of this for only one week of work? So why work when you can drink and dance?! There was no commissar, no one to stop him.

An unlocked car—how could you not steal it, even if you had your own car? On the whole, these Germans didn't understand the Russian individual! What does the Russian need? To get drunk, to get things off his chest! And they...

The Americans who dealt with Narkhov tried to lead him back to good, but it was in vain. Ultimately, Narkhov began to see ghosts when awake and finally understood that he couldn't go on this way. The time had come to go to the embassy, and to re-enter the bosom of the "family."

Now he was in solitary, ate the food served in the camp, and was no longer threatened by the fever of alcohol. He entered solitary confinement* because of a conflict concerning work. He wanted to work at one thing and was forced to work at something else; he refused, was punished, and the same thing happened over again. During the time we spent there, Narkhov was placed twice in the cell for short periods, finished his sentence and left, while we remained.

During those days, the cell still contained joined wooden boards—a great thing, second to none. I slept on the bare wood like a marmot and had very colorful dreams. The cell was relatively warm. Despite hunger, I had a really good time. I learned to ignore it. There was no wake up time and no lights out, no marching or line-ups, no work or counting of prisoners—real joy! Heaven forbid you should wake up even a minute late in the camp when all you had to wake you up was your biological clock. Only in the punishment cells, when I permitted myself to relax on the boards, did I realize how tense I had been up until then.

---

*There are two sorts of imprisonment in the punishment cells; the first: being pent up for several months in cells in which the principal punishment is being denied space and air, and being given worse food; and the second: solitary confinement for a shorter period. The principal punishment in solitary is the harsh starvation and the terrible cold in addition to solitude and the removal of possessions: books, warm clothes, bed, etc.

A Brahmin in solitary

Slava Merkushev, who was not one of my people, had been arrested on the border of Armenia and Turkey, and had been sentenced to ten years for intent to leave the Soviet Union. In Camp 19, he had been immediately influenced by Vandakurov, the great anti–Semite, whom his friends had nicknamed, after his father, "Petrovitch." He claimed that all the world philosophies were "Jewish," and recognized as his ideology something Indian mixed with Nordic paganism and Nazism. He insanely hated the Jews and the anthem he had composed to the Russian "storm troopers" gave evidence of that. Those things were very successful in the camp. Its population was so full of hate that even Wissotsky's* mocking song "Why be considered a criminal and a bandit, it's better to be respected as an anti–Semite..." was seriously accepted. Vandakurov used to sing it in a dark tone accompanied by guitar.

Vandakurov was more serious than those who didn't understand the irony of the song. He incessantly studied philosophy, while searching for means to influence and justify his views. He knew practical (and magical) applications of raja yoga, hypnosis, magic, and felt himself to be a sort of incarnation of the devil on earth. He had a Lucifer-like beard. He dressed up in tight, black clothes and resembled a two-meter-long intestinal worm, with his large, narrow, furious mouth and small, blue eyes. His walk was somewhat bent as he was accustomed to stoop over whoever he was talking with.

Merkushev was totally afraid of him. Without mentioning the name, he told me about someone who had set demons on him. Merkushev described how from his motionlessly recumbent body, a red, partially transparent hand had risen up, and how in the image of a red ghost, he had left his body and observed it from the side. While in this state and with great excitement, he had no desire to return to his body until the demons arrived. First, there were small ones and he easily drove them away, but afterward, the large and strong demon arrived. It attacked him, and shoved itself forcefully into his body, and the red ghost unwillingly and in torment sunk back into Merkushev's body with great opposition. Merkushev sat on his bed in

---

*A folk poet, nationalist, part Jewish.

the middle of the old barrack and wiped cold sweat from his brow. He continued on to India, which he considered his spiritual homeland. Many times he repeated the mantra "I am Brahma, the whole world is Brahma." He was very curious about everything mystical. I sensed that this was all new to him, and that it had overwhelmed him. He was shaken to the depths of his soul, and was incapable of settling these things, incapable of returning to himself. Even his face would suddenly alter unrecognizably, and would express a whole range of characters: from a philosopher to the devil. His words were equally confused and skipped about in volume and clarity from one thing to another. The tension of conflicting forces could be felt in them.

According to him, once, during the noon break on a regular work day, he had been sitting at the table in the cloak room. Suddenly, a shining ray the thickness of a finger had penetrated his head and pulled him to its source. He knew who the ray had been sent from … from some place within the earth, shining numbers, formulas, unknown symbols rose chaotically. He clearly felt that he was being asked for a concealed part of his "self" in exchange, that he relinquish the most precious treasure of his memory. He didn't want to. He was incapable of acquiring wisdom at such a price. From within his conflicted soul, he emitted soundless words, words whose meanings he did not understand:

"Take it, devour it! But the key to the heart's truth lies in Sinai!"

"The key is in my pocket!" answered the evil force and withdrew.

It was difficult to understand the full meaning of his story.

Slava was convinced that a "multi-dimensional struggle" was taking place in the world. There were magician-witches who possessed power and foresaw the future. Every country, every world power was trying to exploit their supernatural talents, to use them as weapons. Since every one of these hypnotists, seers, and magician-witches had varying degrees of superhuman ability, a hierarchy had been created. The struggle among them went on at all levels. Slava didn't reveal everything. From his hints, I understood that this struggle, in his opinion, was happening mainly between the Jews and the Aryans. National borders had no real part in this struggle.

"If this is so, then how is it that I, a Jew, don't know about all this?"

A Brahmin in solitary

Slava would smile slyly and shake with his finger: "You know quite well, but you deny it ... and besides, truth isn't democratic. It is revealed to you as a person who is standing a step higher, by choice and through secret ordination and not by chatter or by means of scrap paper like books."

It was difficult for me to disprove his words because he built everything upon conspiracies of wizardry and not upon solid facts. When a secret is at the center of one's worldview, it is impossible to question it. This was all very Russian. Afterward, he became more moderate and very friendly toward me, offered to teach me yoga and magic. I refused, basing my refusal on the Torah's prohibition.

"As a prisoner, I can't oppose freedom," Slava philosophized, "but as a philosopher, I support a society built like an organism."

At this stage, after we had spent so much time between four walls and a deep bond had formed between us, I told him some of the thoughts that I had on this subject. The organism was composed of smaller living organisms—cells. The individual was like a cell in society. Nevertheless, society was essentially an inferior organism where nothing important occurred aside from primitive metabolism. The unique feature of the organism was its vastly superior level of behavior to that of the cells which composed it. In spite of this, the level of behavior of a state was not superior or wiser at all to that of the individual. The opposite was the case. The state was greater than the individual, but only quantitatively.

Therefore, where was the source of the difference? It lay in the fact that currents of information no less than that in the cells themselves, passed between an organism's cells. In other words, the individual "consciousness" of the cells was open to every other cell. Their reciprocity created the entirety of the organism's consciousness, much higher than that of the individual cell.

The state, on the other hand, united its citizens in a more mechanical manner, epitomized by the army. What administration could coordinate the activities of its subordinates with such art and efficiency, like a harpist coordinating his fingering? In the life of society, the situation was reversed: everything was cumbersome, awkward, and full of inconsistencies, with no direct contact between individuals. Even the simple existence of air surrounding each individual created a sort of obstacle between bodies. In order to transfer information, people needed the resonance created by the organs working mechanically in the body, such as tongue and lips. That fatalistically limited the amount of information transmitted in a unit of time in contrast to the channels which operated immediately and directly within the organism. This was the source of collectivism's defect: people gave up on themselves for the much lower, mechanical (and non-organic) benefit of the whole. The superior being completely sacrificed himself on an inferior altar while tempted by quantitative rather than qualitative characteristics of the mechanical union of organic bodies within society.

Furthermore, society had become more and more a kind of organic body, lacking intellectual activity. As in a uniform body, specializations, reciprocity, flow of materials and information between the various parts of society had multiplied—the more distant we become from the initial condition in which the individual created and supplied himself with the variety of his needs. However, there was no exalted brain over these, which could organize and direct the accumulation of these superhuman forces. As a result, progress carried within it more and more signs of chaos and disintegration. One sign of this was the threat of an ecological holocaust. Humanity's connection to nature was so intensive and diverse, and its outcome so inaccessible for complete consideration, that no human mind could encompass even the basic elements of this critical problem. A multiplicity of minds couldn't effectively coordinate because of the cumbersome channel of communication between them. To stop society's development was also an impossible mission. Anyway, the word "holocaust" expressed it all. There was only one way out of this dead end: to establish direct contact between human minds by radio waves which would become electrical signals in the brain, and the reverse.

Thus it would be possible to circumvent normal conversational channels. Gradually a special language would develop. A language of electrical thoughts, unencumbered by the phonetic symbols of print. It would be equally a complete, rich, and effective language, functioning as a coordinating language between the different body parts. Then, society would become a super-organism, the height of wisdom and perfection unattainable by the solitary individual, just as we are wiser and more perfect than a one-celled creature.

Who knew if such a society would become the seat of God; if a different world would open before it with all the wisdom of the souls who had already departed their bodies? Today's state of science and technology already allowed us to move in that direction, whereas there existed no other system to avoid a holocaust without a miracle. Humanity could function as one super-mind, in comparison to which a single mind would be like one nerve compared to the entire brain. A certain non-technical obstacle would have to be breached: the misanthropy, antipathy and hatred among humans. It would be impossible to merge into one "organism" without mutual affection and attraction.

While I said all of this to Slava, he again felt that the shining ray was penetrating him. He stood next to the door on the cement floor and I walked on the raised board against the background of the barred window. With several magical, circular motions of his hand, the ray was directed toward me, surrounding me from head to foot with a quavering, glowing halo, and Slava already heard my words before I even spoke them! I didn't see all of this, but only felt a gust of the evil wind. I saw his demonic face, constantly changing, and I became silent and closed. In the eyes of my neighbor, the ray, invisible to me, had broken up into shining rings, and they shattered into sparks and disappeared. Everything had gone back to normal.

During our last days together in solitary, Slava intended to flood me with nightmares. Once, I dreamt about a figure of an old woman going up a sloping street at twilight; she radiated a mystical terror, like death itself. However, at that moment, someone seemed to purposely wake me up. I opened my eyes, completely awake, smiled, turned to the other side and again, fell asleep. From then on, nothing terrifying occurred to me in a dream. Slava, who had promised to send me demons when I was awake, was going full steam ahead with his spells, but no demons came.

Jews in the camp

In 1971 the newspapers and journals were full of anti–Semitic poison. Daily, cries were printed of the fearfully mad "court Jews." The media waved about court notices, screaming and barking to fill the void left on the public through state censorship. We too, the Jewish prisoners, had to speak our piece.

We decided to mark the anniversary of the death sentence of the two men accused of plotting to hijack a plane in order to escape from the empire of evil to Israel. With a hunger strike under the slogan "Let my people go!" in preparation, we needed to communicate with the other camps; to transmit information about the free world; to request Israeli citizenship; to prepare an official renunciation of Soviet citizenship. All of this was executed successfully and in complete secret. We were so successful in maintaining secrecy that the Jewish hunger strike of December 24, 1971, began in Camp 19 like a clap of thunder on a clear day.

Before the hunger strike began, a severe flu epidemic had spread throughout the camp. I was in one of the camp's classrooms with a high fever, on my back among many other sufferers. Therefore, I had to get better rapidly in order to have time to act. On the initial day of the hunger strike, I was in a most festive mood. The informers were running about, turning to one side and the other asking how many days we intended to strike. "We'll see," we answered, but the informers weren't satisfied with that. We had prepared for the hunger strike in all areas, including preparation for punitive measures. Even prior to this, I had been informed about the secret order (secret orders were the foundation of life in the camp) to put the hunger strikers to work for the first three days of the strike. That would be a formal way to severely punish them. For one strike day (not going to work), the expected punishment was to remove the right to purchase necessities in the camp's "store" or to receive packages from the outside; for a second day—preventing the prisoner from meeting family members once a year; for a third day—solitary confinement, in a dark, cold cell with no bed or warm apparel. In solitary, you could carry on a hunger strike for as long as you wanted.

In addition to the above measures, "material" piled up about you which could serve as an excuse to send you to Vladimir Prison in the future. Because we knew this, we went to work during the first days of the hunger strike. As difficult as it was, the alternative was worse.

On the fourth day of the hunger strike, they had to send us to medical isolation where there were beds. Because we hadn't disobeyed any order, they couldn't punish us. With me in the same cell were Boris Penson, Harry Kizhner, and Viktor Boguslavsky—who has illustrated this book. The other cells were also occupied. We were lying down on blanket-covered mattresses like kings instead of on bare wood! A new problem arose here. No matter what we talked about, Boris and Viktor changed the subject to food: where, with whom, and when they had eaten something tasty, something delicious.

"Guys, better let's talk about women!" However, on the fifth day of a hunger strike, the subject of women didn't have much value. Even if Viktor began to tell about some personal affair, he immediately switched the subject and went back to talking about food: what and how she had cooked something, etc.

Three times a day, the guard brought food to the cell and left it there under our noses from morning to night. In the adjacent cell, Lev Yagman began to suffer a heart attack. The cell was almost hermetically sealed and was terribly crowded, and the guard refused to allow even a small opening for air.

"Red Nazis!" those of us who still had a bit of strength shouted. We pounded on the door and demanded a doctor. We pressured Lev to end his hunger strike, but to no avail. With our last bit of strength, we sang "Jerusalem of Gold."

Noone of us broke down. We all lasted exactly seven days. The moment we declared an end to the hunger strike, we were sent, without pause, back to backbreaking work.

The operating methods of the KGB

In our camp, a war criminal, who had been among those recruited into the German police in the conquered territory and who had taken part in the annihilation of the Jews, shouted horribly in his sleep. In the morning, he refused to talk about what he had dreamt. "I don't remember," he said, but his desperate, terrified shouting resumed again at night. His neighbor, who was woken up by the shouting, saw a vague shadow bending over this sleeping murderer and it grabbed him by the throat to strangle him…

An Ukrainian, who in the past had fought for Ukrainian independence, had KGB agents poisoning his food. This happened after his release from the camp (something that occurred repeatedly). He was walking with a friend in the street when he suddenly fell down. His body grew cold. Afterward, he related how he had viewed his body hovering above him after he had fallen! He floated, transparent and bodiless, rising higher and higher and people were gathering below and an ambulance arrived. He rose above the houses; the sky darkened until it was completely black. He flew and rose higher and higher. A weak light flickered above him. Gradually the light became focused and appeared as two stars. The dead man flew toward them. The stars became larger until they turned into two angels. They took him by the hand and he sensed the words "your time has not yet come." The angels carried him below, and the darkness began to grow lighter, and everything became totally illumined. He saw houses, streets, people, and the ambulance. In the midst of the crowd, a nurse in a white coat inserted a syringe into a vein in an arm of his inert body. For another moment, he viewed this scene from up above, and suddenly he returned to himself. He saw the nurse's face bending directly above him. His atheistic friend, who had been witness to this clinical death and who he had told about his return to a cold body, then became a believer.

The operating methods of the KGB

Luck was not on the side of the prisoner Baranov, from the Russian nationalist group who also had been released. On his way from the camp, after having first drunk in the company of some "friend," his heart stopped forever. He was one of those who tended not to cooperate with the KGB.

Russian Christianity always had the tendency to formal superficiality. Therefore, to this day, there are villages of witches and warlocks. Sometimes, these also existed in the cities. In the camps, of course, the issue of magic became more intense. I had the opportunity of hearing how the person on-duty in the hut, a "polizei,"* with a saccharine red face, engaged in whispering when he opened the oven. Whispers that were a prayer to the devil, magic. Afterward, at Vladimir Prison, a young, clear-skinned, blue-eyed deserter from the Soviet army, Bogdan Veduta, told me how one witch had tried to recruit him to be his student. It turned out that the KGB had made contact with people like that in an attempt to use their skill for their own purposes. In exchange, they were given various additional privileges. However, the warlock hardly spoke about this sensitive subject and was miserly with facts.

As already related, once, when I was in solitary, I experienced the world beyond with all my being. This had been an experience so full of light and joy, that I could then doubt the existence of hell. However, the belief in hell was dictated by a terror which was difficult to describe, and actual flesh and blood demons, of which I had seen more than enough. Among them were those for whom their spice of life was to cause harm to everyone around them. In the juicy jargon of the camps, it was said that "he breathes out poison." Belief is only belief, but once I actually did experience the meaning of hell.

I woke up in the middle of the night and felt in terror that I could not move. I couldn't feel my body. Some terrible and frightening force crushed me into a dark abyss. I couldn't describe in human language this nameless condition of mystical and crushing terror. With all its strength, my spirit strove to free itself from this mute strangulation

---

*Police, collaborators with the Nazis during World War II, who also participated in mass executions in the Nazi-occupied territories in World War II.

The Guards Spoke Russian

of devastation. I couldn't think about anything, I couldn't remember the words of prayer. In silence, without a sound, the awful struggle continued. It was something like what happens in arm wrestling, when each person places his elbow on the table and tries to pin down his opponent's arm, but for a long time the arms remain even, full of the hard tension of the struggle, still and petrified.

However, the hostile force had begun to withdraw. Gradually, there was relief. I had overcome it! With a horrible, desperate sob of helpless anger, the dark force had been overcome and withdrew. I felt my body again, opened my eyes with ease, and raised myself up a bit. Everyone around me was sleeping. That is, no one had heard this loud sob, no one had shouted out in their sleep. Next to me, in the neighboring bed, Alex Halperin lightly snored. Dawn a warlock rose past the window and soon the wake up signal would sound. Just a minute. So where did I hear that nasal voice? Was that voice heard in the heart of the anti–Semitic circle in the spirit of "The Black Hundred?"* Wasn't that the voice coming from behind me in one of the line-ups, a snake's hiss, "You-u-u, f...cking Jew!"? Yes, it was you, a flesh and blood Satan, resembling a giant intestinal worm! You didn't succeed! "Husk"—that's your true name! That's the term kabalah uses for the soot of the fire of being.

Prisoners' pathologies

Despite all the isolation in the camps, the prisoners heard information about what was happening in the other camps. In Camp 10, nicknamed "striped" because of its inmates' striped uniforms, there was a prisoner nicknamed "General Bezukhov" (earless). He had received this nickname because he had cut off and sent his ears to one of the party committees, with the explanation that he was

---

*A general name for the anti–Semitic organization in Russia in the beginning of the 20th century and especially after 1905, which received support from the tsarist regime and which organized street battles against democrats and socialists, and pogroms against Jews.

sick and tired of hearing their stupid chatter. Due to his recklessness, Bezukhov was kept in the punishment cells of the concentration camp in solitary confinement.

There he lay, naked on the exposed boards because he used to tear his clothes to pieces (as well as anything else possible) and swallow them, buttons included. Even in winter, he always broke the window of his cell and slept under it. In the morning he woke up on the bench covered in snow, and then he stood and stretched. Steam rose from his red, naked body. His breath ascended like smoke from the stovepipe. He was taken out to the latrine. On the way, there was a bucket with bleach for sanitizing the slop bucket so that it wouldn't smell too much.

"General Bezukhov" filled a ladle with the bleach, moved his mouth toward it, drank, grunted, and went on his way.

Anatoly Marchenko described in great detail the self-inflicted tortures of the prisoners and how they ate parts of their bodies after they had cut them off. I also heard similar stories, about how prisoners tried to get to the camp hospital in order to avoid slave labor for a time, as well as to receive better rations compared to the usual camp food. The doctor-guards stopped reacting to instances of swallowed domino tiles, knowing that the prisoner would ultimately eliminate them in the bathroom.

Despite this, how could a prisoner get to the hospital for expected surgery and its accompanying rest under such difficult circumstances? What was to be done?

A prisoner came to the doctor and said to him: "I swallowed an iron pin from the train tracks (meaning the large pin which joins the iron train track to the edge of the rail)."

No one believed him and he was led to the x-ray machine, and there it was—an iron pin! How was it possible to swallow such a thing? And there indeed was a story like that: the "sword swallower" had smoothed the sides of the pin to make them round, rubbed them with solidol so the pin would slip down easily, lifted his face with raised jaw, so that his throat and mouth would become one straight, continuous canal, into which he then slowly lowered the pin, head facing downward.

The Guards Spoke Russian

Often there were pathologies connected to the long absence of a sex life in camp. The criminal Titov had been sent to Vladimir Prison because he had ambushed a teacher in a hallway after she came in from outside. He fell upon her and after touching her skirt, he felt complete sexual satisfaction. In prison he practiced exhibitionism and did this each time the nurse opened the slot in his door. However, this was only the first rung on the ladder of pathology. Another criminal prisoner in Vladimir Prison gained renown by cutting his penis and throwing it through the window when the prison's female health administrator, Helena Nikolayevna Botova (the Ilse Koch of Vladimir Prison)* was walking by. It was hard to accept that someone could do something to his body, like shoving an "anchor," something like a multiple fishhook, into his urethra.

These phenomena were perhaps anchored in the national personality. Psychologists say that a person who doesn't love himself is dangerous to those around him. What can be said about those whose lack of self-love has reached an immeasurable level?

This riddle held the solution to another riddle: how did such a disorganized people, not unified, drunk and sloppy, who knew no bounds, manage to overcome all its neighbors step by step, and over their corpses establish the largest empire in the world, not by a miracle, not by short-lived efforts, but over hundreds of years of expansion and relentless shoving of their feet through the door? Did they manage to conquer the world due to some particular quality?

That unstoppable force was the same one which led to these terrible self-inflicted tortures. That was the Russian demon. It had amazing power, both attractive and paralyzing. It swallowed things like a swamp, like a monster's maw. It digested things like a furnace.

It was for a good reason that the true Russian folk poet (whose poems the Russian people knew, cherished, and sang with special nostalgia), Sergei Yesenin, had been the poet of grief, wanton licentiousness, destruction and devastation; the poet of death's terrible beauty. Like death itself, his people marched onward, with fire and

---

*Ilse Koch was the wife of Karl Koch, commander of the Buchenwald concentration camp and the Maidenek extermination camp in Poland. She was infamous because of her sadistic behavior toward the prisoners.

sword, destroying everything in their path, strangling thought in the bud, while seeing and hearing only their yearning, only their soul quenched by the drug of death. They went on to wonder: why did all the others complain, oppose, and defend their own miserable interests? Could anything compare to that hell they carried inside?

It seemed that they themselves were guilty of everything. "The Russian 'muzhik' has it worse than anyone else..." but it was worse for him only because instead of there being normal order in his house, he preferred a glass of vodka and a chauvinist dance of demons to a crust of bread, preferring to slaughter, strangle and rape others replete with happiness in order to "save ... the whole ungrateful world...." For some reason, the victims needed to feel compassion for the wandering bandit, freezing within the forest, who lay in wait for prey on the highways instead of working his field in peace and contentment, a field so big that it had enough for ten people.

Only a few Russians wanted to learn the story of the Jewish people under Russian rule, which for hundreds of years had tortured and tormented the Jews with a hundred and fifty discriminatory laws and trials outside the bounds of any humane law, before they began to think about the number of Jews who had been in the ranks of the revolutionaries.

The accusation that "the Jews made the Revolution" must be answered, because the Russians pushed the Jews to the Revolution, and not only the Russians. I don't want to go into length on the subject, because for all of the claims against the Jews, there is a single true and unbeatable response: if they had taken you, my dear sirs, uprooted you from your homeland, pursued you for thousands of years as if you were an animal in the woods, it would behoove you to stop, look, and see what would become of you, and then, make comparisons.

However, under no circumstance would we have treated them the same. We simply don't have the same brutality, not even a hundredth of it. I don't want to slide over quietly the unjustified accusations and claims against other enslaved peoples, who apparently abused innocent Russia.

Who slaughtered the Hungarians in 1848? Who abused Poland? Who drowned the Chinese as if they were puppies in the river during

The Guards Spoke Russian

the Russo-Japanese War? Who enslaved Latvia, the Caucasus, the Ukraine, and a hundred or two hundred other peoples throughout hundreds of years? Who profited from all that? Who was the only one in the 20th century to retain a colonial empire? Who increased their population, not by births, but by conquering other peoples? And who, in spite of this, had lost a considerable part of its people inside barbed wire fences or through organized starvation? Who stands on the brink of national death?

Russia, especially in its prisons and camps, was fertile soil for the flourishing of different pathologies. The individual there was attacked on all sides, and above all, was threatened by an atmosphere of suspicion, great tension, and cruel evil, dark and heavy like lead.

In the exiles' pamphlet "@Grani," one of the Russian oppositionists described how an adult had responded in the subway to a child who hadn't relinquished his seat to somebody: "I would tear out your eyes." That is very typical. One of the guards in the camp wrote a report about a prisoner whose family name was Dana: "He slept next to the train embankment for an unknown purpose."

It was particularly terrible to suddenly find yourself under the crushing steamroller of the camp without any spiritual support, without religious books, with nothing. A man who stood on the edge of the abyss needed support like air to breathe. Because he had no such support, he had to somehow build a spiritual edifice from within his soul, in haste, from whatever spiritual junk was at hand.

The simplest way was to find a victim, to grasp on to something anti-. Anti-Semitism, for example. That earned encouragement from above. Added to this were physical problems, such as intense sexual starvation over many years. For example, many partisans had fallen into the hands of the Chekists (the members of the NKVD, the earlier incarnation of the KGB) while they were young. They had grown older in the camp without once having touched a woman. All around them, they saw only grey prison coveralls and guard uniforms with epaulets red as blood! Some of them couldn't even watch a movie, and they would faint when they saw a "real" woman on the screen...

The hunger for vitamins and protein, the hunger for quality and quantities of food eroded strength through the years, dried up the mind, caused nervous system collapse, and created slow, irreversible, pathological changes in the human body. We must not forget the disciplinary measures, based upon inexhaustible evil and stealth, impossible to adapt to, but any deviation from discipline drew infinite punishments. The prisoner lived on the razor's edge.

To all of these were added the pressures of family, the attempts to fragment it, the cancellation of rare visits, being fired from work, stealing letters, spreading malicious rumors and gossip, veiled threats ... enough to make one crazy.

"We are like a fly whose blood is sucked by the spider," an old Estonian prisoner used to say to me. He meant that visibly the fly was intact, and only its dead outer shell remained.

Corruption

A former Ukranian partisan was carrying an electric engine from place to place. He stopped and wiping away his sweat, sat down next to me on the bench. "I only lugged this little thing, and already I'm totally wet and trembling, like in a fever...."

Another lad sat forlorn and there was an unnatural melancholy in his cloudy eyes.

"What happened to you?"

"I can't get any tea. I was used to it. Don't you have any?"

"How would I have any?"

The most concentrated tea was a substitute for vodka in the camp. There were two sources of tea: the guards-profiteers and the KGB special department. Tea was sold in the camp covertly at a price ten times greater than the store price, and sometimes in exchange for a prisoner's food ration. This narcotic longing was a sure path to the arms of the special department. If you became an informer or provocateur, you would receive unlimited packages of tea. In exchange for special services provided to the KGB, certain prisoners were released before serving half their sentences. The boy who had been looking for tea became one of them.

Other tea fanciers, the more well off, weren't connected directly to the KGB, but to all sorts of dubious groups and had to tolerate them in order to enjoy the tea they obtained in mysterious ways.

However, these groups didn't only deal in tea drinking and the "conversations" accompanying it. The KGB had set a clear goal: to corrupt the political prisoner any way possible and to destroy him as an opponent.

There was an ugly character in Camp 19 named Kurnikov, and nicknamed "Hitler." He was thin, with protruding bones, dark skin. Resembling a demon, he was apparently one of the criminal prisoners, and among the worst of them. He spoke in a very characteristic tone, drawing out and lazily pronouncing each syllable. He worked in the furnace room, felt like he owned it, and lived with a fat prisoner who resembled a woman. In our narrow circle, he was nicknamed "Eva Braun." Things were done openly, even demonstrably, and the guards only helped in this, allowing them a joint work space where they could close themselves off—a rare privilege. The aim of this treatment was to tempt "hungry" prisoners. According to Soviet law, homosexuality was a punishable crime. However, nothing threatened "Hitler." And there were those who were tempted.

Here's a story of one of the prisoners. One night he woke up, and before he understood what was happening, he felt a strange hand feeling around in his undergarments. Terrified, he turned over on his back and covered himself well with his blanket. Nausea and helplessness washed over him, along with an unclear desire to kill his benchmate or to escape to the forbidden section next to the camp fence, a target for the guards' bullets. It also happened that passive homosexuals endlessly harassed prisoners who initially didn't understand why this person had latched on to them—was he an informer, or what?

"Hitler" had previously done a stint in the "striped" camp, and dealt there in drug smuggling. He and his gang of criminal prisoners used to sit in a closed cell and smoke hashish. Even those who didn't want the drug had to inhale it. Generally, a young and fresh prisoner would be thrown to Hitler and his partners, and they made sure to move him down the assembly line: drugs, cards, homosexuality, until the man had been erased. Then, it was as if he hadn't existed, unless the investigating officer wanted to use him a bit longer, while waving the criminal clause for the crime of homosexual relations in his face.

The path of the "new one" came to a rapid end and a new victim would be thrown to "Hitler."

Afterward, when he was in Camp 35 (in the Urals), "Hitler" compiled a gang of thugs, and moved on to the use of real physical force under the administration's orders, using direct terror against the political prisoners.

The liberators are coming!

A young Ukrainian named Mikola Horbal was arrested because of his stubborn adherence to his mother tongue, and his ballads—"thoughts"—which he wrote and which no one else read. Once in a store, his friend asked him in Russian for matches. Mikola corrected the name of the product and said it in Ukrainian, annoyed because he had a terrible feeling that his language was "being dried up." During the interrogation, the KGB man offered him a cigarette. "Here are matches, oh, excuse me," and the interrogator translated the word from Russian to Ukrainian in a meaningful tone and looked with hate into Mikola's eyes.

"Which of the *banderovtsi** taught you? This? Or maybe this?" and the KGB man shoved one picture after another of horrible, tortured corpses in front of the prisoner's face. Twenty years prior, the NKVD agents had thrown corpses such as these, bloated, tortured, their eyes gouged out, into western Ukraine's town squares and emphatically forbade covering them up and burying them so that others would see and be seen, in order to dissuade future partisans. They didn't even

---

*Nationalist Ukrainian partisans.

give the dead peace: each corpse was desecrated by a spear and/or its eyes were gouged by a boot heel. If that was how they treated the dead, what could be expected from them in their treatment of the living?

I had seen the pulverized fingers of Bogdan Cheviko, one of the members of the Ukrainian underground. KGB agents had crushed his bones in the door, one by one, during interrogation. Even those who had been given the death sentence had been tortured. Heritz Herchak, who had been sentenced to death when he was very young, would then be moved from cell to cell, and each time was a kind of execution. Despite his young age, his hair turned white because of the emotional and physical abuse he had undergone.

"You should learn a lesson," said the torturers while performing their deed. Every night, the click of boots was heard on the floor. Perhaps they were coming to take you? No, they were going to the neighboring cell. And thus it went on, for months.

Scissors weren't given to those sentenced to death. The guards trimmed their fingernails. They cut the fingernails of one of the partisan commanders along with the flesh. They cut his hair in the same manner. He returned from the "ceremony" covered in blood.

The Lithuanian partisan, Piatras Pukinskas was so harshly tortured by the KGB that he frequently lost consciousness. While they were trying to bring him to life, the Russian female translator amused herself by stomping on him, trying to hurt his groin with her sharp heels.

Toward the end of the partisan struggle in the Ukraine, the combatants hid in bunkers which were difficult to gain access to. The KGB tried to recruit foresters, hunters, and others who lived alone in the forest and knew it well, so that with their assistance, they could get to the last, more cautious partisans. The recruits supplied the partisans with winter clothes, and prior to giving them the clothes, they injected the clothing with a special substance according to KGB instructions. Afterward, typhus lice developed in the clothing and the inhabitants of entire bunkers died without a fight.

One of the foresters had been uncovered, so they set an ambush. But he also died from typhus (perhaps not by chance—after all, he was an unneeded witness). The informers "feted" the less cautious

The liberators are coming!

partisans with large doses of sleeping potions in their food. One of the Ukrainians told me that all of the partisans who tasted this food, served to them in one of the homes, fell like sheaves after harvest. He had been stronger and left the house. He saw the approaching KGB agents through the mist. He took out his gun and wanted to lift it to shoot and to shout. Instead, he fell on the roadway. The partisans who had been captured woke up in the interrogation rooms as if disabled. One was half blind, one had a damaged leg, the sleeping substance was that strong.

The KGB used to approach the relatives of the partisans who had not yet been captured. "Mother!" they would shout. "Mother! Save your son! Otherwise we'll shoot him! Help!"

The women who didn't agree to cooperate were severely beaten. Thus it happened that a mother herself would add a sleeping potion to the food and turn her son over to the KGB. She didn't know that by doing this, she was sending him to twenty-five years of hell, compared to which death was a blessing.

Afterward, the KGB moved on to more subtle methods. The same Horbal related that when he was once in a sanatorium, a Russian girl invited him to sail on the river. He refused. Many of the talented and creative Ukrainian youths were gathered there that day. Another Ukrainian girl agreed to the proposed outing instead of Horbal. She never returned from the outing. She had drowned. They said the boat had turned over and apparently, and despite the fact that the girl who had drowned was an excellent swimmer, and despite the fact that the girl who had done the inviting didn't know how to swim; in spite of all that, the latter was the one who returned healthy and hale. "I was the one who was supposed to drown!" was the thought that had occurred to him.

That was the system of "pruning the buds"—the young, talented nationalists—before they could develop, gain renown, and have their say. A known example was the murder of Alla Horsky, a Ukrainian artist. Here and there nationalist talents were killed in car accidents, river drownings, falling into the hands of unidentified ruffians. Everything was done quietly, without identifying marks. Entire gangs of young, well-trained KGB agents operated in western Ukrainian cities, and in Kiev too.

The Guards Spoke Russian

In Lithuania after the war, in the first years of the Russian Communist occupation, the situation had been no different. Those who hadn't wanted to join the partisans were forced by the situation to do so: soldiers and KGB attacked every young farmer, beat him brutally and shouted "You too are a bandit (a gang member). Where are the rest?!"

This was no life. It would have been preferable to flee to the forest. Every night there were new explosions, fires, robberies, murders, rapes. The soldiers even raped murdered women, and raped children. When Lithuania was independent, the Poles weren't happy because of a conflict over the capital city. However, when the Soviets came, the Poles helped the Lithuanian partisans even though they hadn't forgotten their territorial claims. But as for Russian immigrants after the Revolution they got along excellently in independent Lithuania. No one persecuted them, and they were well treated. Over dozens of years of an independent Lithuania, the Russian minority learned to speak Lithuanian and acclimated well. The Russian immigrants used this knowledge after the war (after Lithuania had been occupied by the Soviets and had lost their independence), when they cooperated with the KGB and joined the special anti-partisan divisions that were then established.

Initially, it had been easy for the Lithuanians to identify danger in their hiding places. If they heard words in Lithuanian, they knew it was one of theirs and they could get out. If they heard Russian, they knew that they had to hide and prepare for battle because those voices were either soldiers or the KGB. However, the special divisions, "the destroyers" as they were called then, completely exploited this innocence.

The Estonians had fought for hundreds of years against German expansionist aspirations. Even during Russian tsarist rule, the burden of the German nobles had been too heavy, and Estonian hatred had been turned against them. During the war for independence, the Estonians had fought with all their might against the Germans. The rifle barrels caught fire from so much use until it was impossible to fire them. Then, the Estonians attacked the Germans in face-to-face combat and struck them with their flaming rifles as if they were sticks. The Bolsheviks came for only a year, the year that preceded the Hitler-Stalin war, and a miracle occurred. They "forced" the Estonians and the Latvians to love the Germans!

This one year was so awful that its horrors outweighed all the iniquities of the Crusaders. Generally, occupiers exterminate a certain portion of the occupied people, but the Bolsheviks had determined to hurt both the heart and the brain. They destroyed and vandalized the most delicate and vital buildings of the national organism, its soul, its will, its conscience.

It is easy for us to understand this because of our experience: the splendid Russian Judaism of Lubavitch, Jabotinsky, and Bialik turned into dough under the red boots, devoid of faith and tradition, culture and language. They hastened to destroy the rabbis first of all, the Zionists, the Hebrew teachers, and even the *mohels*—entire strata that concentrated the nation's identity.

The camps were full of those who opposed the Bolshevik monster, of those who had defended their land, their relatives, their lives, their people, their homes, their country, their right to speak their mother tongue, to speak about what they held dear, to believe in what they wanted to believe. With typical communist cynicism, these people were sentenced to prison terms of 25 years for "all of the Motherland!"

Whoever had been born and had grown up in an independent Lithuania, had served in its army, had sworn loyalty to it, and had been its citizen, was accused of "betrayal of the Muscovite" Motherland, the Soviet state as the mother of all. Know this, traitors, wherever you're hiding! Punishment is inevitable! Not in vain did this joke make the rounds: in the Soviet encyclopedia, the entry for "elephants" appears under the title "the Soviet Union is the birthplace of elephants," meaning that everything has been originated in the Soviet Union.

When I thought about this indescribable brutality, I recollected one of the criminal prisoners who sat with me in the same cell during my incarceration. He had been a regular construction worker who had finished his army service and participated in the occupation of Czechoslovakia, which he felt had been unjust.

It is fitting here to note that in Soviet Russia, all kinds of theft were a matter of routine. In shops or slaughterhouses, dining rooms and restaurants, this was figured into the worker's stipulated salary. "If you don't steal—you won't live." This history of theft, bribery, and corruption had been going on in an uninterrupted chain since the days of Ivan the Terrible. This was even convenient for the despotic state. Everyone was held in a tight fist, at any moment it was possible to punish anyone using a legal pretext. Because of this, the average citizen had to keep quiet and know his place.

And this lad, this construction worker, kept quiet. Meanwhile, together with his friends, he gradually stole building materials. With the profits, he drank and got drunk. That was the norm in those days. Then his group encountered a little idealistic communist, a difficult breed to find. The latter suddenly appeared, began to inform and ruined everything. They tried to persuade him, warned him, threatened him, but to no avail.

Then, something terrible happened. They invited the little communist into a house trailer where the construction workers lived. Together, they attacked him and beat him with fists and feet. When he lay on the floor motionless, the group had a nice idea. They started tossing him up in the air so that each time he fell, he hit the floor. This of course caused fracturing and tearing of all his internal bodily systems. The victim died suffering terribly.

A short time afterward, the members of the group began to appear secretly at the police station, one by one. Each of them wanted to be the first to tell and put the blame on the others. This also showed that the gang was made up of ordinary people, that the relationships in it were not firm. They were all young workers who had never been previously arrested. My cellmate also wasn't anyone special. He was physically healthy and liked to laugh; his head was round, that's all. And of course, he had no worries or misgivings.

In Camp 19, occasionally the guards organized a cat hunt. This was one of their many "cultural activities." A huge guard, a mountain of a man, nicknamed "Ivan and a half," walked about the camp, grabbed the poor animals and shoved them into a sack. When the sack was full, the guard went to the furnace room and threw the full sack into the burning furnace. Terrible blood-curdling yowls of the cats being burned alive came from inside the furnace. Even the former Nazi crematoria workers would flee.

Divide and rule

Against the backdrop of the mass quarrels and slayings inspired by the rule of the criminal prisoners, political prisoners didn't abstain from "self-destruction." The national divisions among the political prisoners were exploited. Arguments were stirred up among them with the help of agents and informers who provided knives and spread rumors: "Ukrainian brothers, the Latvians are planning to slaughter us! Arm yourselves! X is already dead. The Letts did it!"

Meanwhile, the exact same thing was said to the Latvians. And when you looked around you could see that they really were arming themselves, and their looks spread terror. That being the case: get prepared! Sharpen the knives! Thus, blood was spilled and hundreds of hot heads and mere passers-by fell, "done in by the knife." When someone had to defend himself, there was no joking around. Those who joked met with a bitter end.

The more level-headed political prisoners had experience and knew how to distinguish an agent and catch him "red-handed," revealing the plot. For the most part, however, it was usually too late. Blood had already been spilled. Each person lost a friend or a brother, among people already divided by hatred, suspicion, and revenge.

After having sown loathing among the enslaved, slavery prospered. Why feel compassion for prisoners, if to achieve the "grand idea" of equality of all men, such things, and even worse, had yet been done? More than once, KGB units had masqueraded as nationalist partisans and had done terrible things in their name. In Byelorussia, during World War II, special divisions of the KGB had dressed in S.S. uniforms and had roamed about the villages, burning, robbing and raping.

Then the people turned to the forests. The population had been

The Guards Spoke Russian

accustomed to surrendering without complaint to any regime and it was difficult to arouse their wrath. Nothing similar to the undergrounds of Greece, Yugoslavia, or Poland took place in the territories of the Soviet Union conquered by the Germans. The difference between tyrants was in the length of the dictator's mustache: Stalin's was longer, and Hitler's was shorter. In contrast, the demagoguery and methods were almost identical. Therefore, the Germans easily managed to bring over to their side nearly a million Russian soldiers while their homeland was bleeding in the war against the Germans.

How would there be pity for foreign prisoners in Russia, when millions of soldiers drunk on vodka, were led by Soviet commanders to certain death facing the machine guns? The German positions were amazed to find themselves surrounded by drunk soldiers, who attacked in waves over the piles of the corpses of those who had preceded them. I heard this from an old Estonian, who, in revenge, enlisted to fight against the reds.

However, in my time, under Brezhnev's regime, things did not reach actual slaughter. The methods of reciprocal incitement also had proved themselves to be less and less effective. "The big warlock" Vandakurov, was the center for inciting the nationalist Russians. He already had one escape against him and he walked about in a blue sweater, when wearing a civilian garment by other prisoners aroused the guards' hysterical reaction and the implementation of emergency actions. He and his buddies tried to redirect the natural hatred of the hangmen toward the Jews, who had already proved themselves as the most stable and efficient base of opposition to the authorities in the camp. The Jewish groups were those who arranged the frequent dissemination of information from the camps. This image of the Jew was earmarked by the authorities for the devil. There was no need to dig especially deep in order to discover the KGB's guiding hand.

A sad tale was told about Vandakurov. Once he sat in prison with a partially criminal prisoner (a prisoner who had committed "common" criminal acts as well as political crimes) nicknamed "the Count," who very much wanted to be free. Vandakurov managed to persuade him that he could teach him how to move through walls by magic. "You have no body. The 'zhids' have worked hard four thousand years to persuade people to believe that they have a body. You have no body!"

In order to be purified from the Jewish influence of thousands of years, the Count had to strictly fast for a long time. Vandakurov generously agreed to take his food ration. After some time, the Count became so thin that the wall no longer seemed to be an impassable obstacle…

"It's still too soon!" Vandakurov restrained him and dissuaded him from taking the decisive step.

"No, that's it… I feel that I'm ready," the emaciated Count faced the wall…

"Here, you see, didn't I tell you it was too soon!" Vandakurov assured the Count. It seemed that the Count had begun to understand. He grabbed a kettle and attacked Vandakurov, doing no harm because he was too weak.

Under these camp conditions, people reached such degrees of madness that one person declared himself to be Jesus, and another to be his mother, Mary, and a third, the archangel Michael. Judomania was particularly rife. Suddenly, Shepshelovitch was prevented from having a family reunion, after his mother had taken the trouble to come from faraway Latvia.

In reaction, nearly all the prisoners in the camp announced a hunger strike! This disrupted the authorities' regular program of inciting the political prisoners against each other, according to nationality. Since this strike, two decisive main opposition forces stood out in the camp: Jews and Ukrainians. This became the custom from then on: if Jews and Ukrainians said "yes"—the operation had been guaranteed. The KGB went crazy. They began to summon the Ukrainian youth, one by one, and attacked them with insane shouts.

"What are you doing with those 'zhids'?"

"And which of us is an internationalist?" responded the Ukrainians with an ironic question. The authorities began to fear that the enslaved peoples would find a common language in the "big camp," the entire Soviet Union, surrounded by its barbed wire. That would be a catastrophe, because in the "big camp," the clever policy of inciting one people against another was the cornerstone of the empire's existence.

The slave mentality

I remember that something incomprehensible instilled me with a feeling of terrible depression when I heard the conversations of certain prisoners with guards. They didn't talk about anything special, only "life." I didn't immediately understand that it was the intimacy of the tone that unconsciously bothered me.

In an unclear, pathological manner, the hangman and the victim had become father and son, and indeed, this incomprehensible matter was what Russia lived and breathed. This was a psychological phenomenon of natural tyranny, where people were incapable of even imagining in their most secretive dreams a form of mutual relationship other than that of hangman and victim. A person could be dissatisfied with his place in this system, or with a certain condition, but not with the system itself, because it had become a part of his essence.

A proud Byelorussian, Ostrayekov was his name, asked me, "Have you noticed that they [the Russians] prefer the company of nationalities other than their own, despite all their xenophobia?"

I had noticed it, but I didn't know the reason for it.

"For the most part, their character is a very difficult one—angry, domineering, and cruel. When they meet each other, it's like 'a scythe against a stone'; they can't live together. On the other hand, the others are more tolerant. They give in here, they soothe there, sometimes they'll act as if they didn't hear—it's easier to get along that way!"

Ostrayekov smiled broadly, satisfied with his skill of discernment.

To be fair, I'll say that in Russia there are also many types of people devoid of character, who are submissive, easy to sway, looking to where or with whom they can find refuge. However, people who are level-headed, stable, restrained and sober are a minority.

I tried to stay in the barrack as little as possible, not only because of the cramped atmosphere, but also because of its spiritual atmosphere. I escaped to a place where there were fewer people and more greenery, to a place where only blue skies and green forests grew and darkened, as seen through the fence.

The surprise

One of the most surprising things in the political camps was the friendly treatment to the Zionists by us Ukrainian nationalists.

This had great, at times decisive, importance. Because the Ukrainians made up nearly half of the political prisoners, their influence was also great with the other nationalist communities, imprisoned like them because of their opposition to the Russian occupation. This wasn't only lip service, but active identification and participation in protests for mutual defense in the face of persecution.

In Camp 35 in the Urals, in the Perm district, when the criminal element incited by the KGB tried to organize a pogrom against the Zionist community, the Ukrainians stopped them and threatened: "If you touch the Jews, you'll have us to deal with!"

The rioters were frightened. They had good reason to flinch. The veteran partisans, who had fought Hitler and Stalin, weren't just bandying words.

The Ukrainian political prisoners—both the partisans as well as the young, educated ones—were mostly positive and pleasant, very far from the common stereotype. In ideological discussions it became clear that the root of the hostility between the two peoples, the Ukrainians and the Jews, lay in their enslavement of, and by, east and west, which for several hundred years had seen that the two peoples fight each other and leave the enslaver alone.

The Guards Spoke Russian

A Polish nobleman in Ukraine ensured that a padded layer of court Jews would divide him from his oppressed vassals, making the Jews responsible for collections. When the Ukrainians erupted with rebellions of terrible despair, the rulers often bought their immunity by handing over the Jews to the rebels for punishment. The communists also made sure that during the annihilation of the Ukrainian people in the organized starvation of 1933, the names of Jewish collaborators would stand out in the leadership ranks. On the other hand, the dirtiest positions in the persecution of the "cosmopolites" and the Zionists were reserved for Ukrainian collaborators.

The dependency of the Jewish people on the ruler originated with being an exiled people, denied rights, and being given to the benevolence of their neighbors. Thus, the Jew appeared to the occupied and oppressed peoples as the loyal assistant of the ruler. Jewish youth were en masse swept away by communism in the period of the Revolution. A merciless regime crushing the individual, his body, soul, and possessions, made the situation immeasurably worse and "contributed" to the Holocaust wherever communism ruled or threatened.

However, the moment the Ukrainians encountered the Zionists, who were seeking to break away from Moscow, they perceived them as a friendly factor, taking to them enthusiastically. Knowing the history before enslavement, this phenomenon is unsurprising. Kiev was the only European capital whose ruler, similar to the Khazars, tested out Judaism as one of the possibilities for his people in the process of breaking away from their pagan tradition.

These Ukrainian prisoners erased the disgrace of the enslavement of the political prisoners to the camp underworld. They destroyed the fear of the informers. They organized and led the rebellion of the 1950s in Kolyma, in Vorkuta, and in Karaganda. These were particularly rough areas because of the climate, or because of the hard labor. It was there where a vast number of prisoners had been concentrated. They stood bare-handed facing the machine guns, the tanks crushing everything in their path, including humans, in the face of the army bombers. Even after 25 years of life in hell, many of them remained pure in spirit, despite the absence of all hope.

The hand of fate united these two nationalities, the Ukrainians

The surprise

and the Jews, as first in Moscow's list to be annihilated. This was felt not only in the camps. The quantitative ratio between Russians to Ukrainians in the Soviet empire at the beginning of the Revolution was 1.5:1 and now it stood at 3:1. Approximately 11 million Russians flooded into Ukraine, which had been emptied of nearly a half of its original inhabitants through starvation, collectivization, and the mass purges. Most of those remaining feared opening their mouth in their mother tongue. There are those who have said that even at the time these lines were written, most of the white population of Siberia and the Caucasus consists of Ukrainian exiles and their offspring.

Likewise, Jews in the Russian empire numbered approximately five million. By now there should have been at least ten million. However, we must be grateful if there are a million left. Even those generally lacking Jewish identity who have assimilated. The number of mixed marriages among them, generation after generation, threatens the uniqueness of the people, and perhaps may even create a third mixed nationality.

The Jews are in this position because of the mass annihilation of all the layers of Judaism in the Soviet Union, in which they had preserved their national identity, their immunity, their strength and all that they represented.

In 1953, in the latter part of the "doctors' plot," organized pogroms were planned. Those who survived them were supposed to be sent to the most terrible parts of Siberia, as was done to the Chechnyans and several other nationalities.

Large barracks with no walls on two sides were built at the destinations. In the Siberian winter, the meaning of this was clear: certain death without having to waste any zyklon gas. The transport trains, like those of the Holocaust, waited at all the stations. Only a Purim miracle—the death of the enemy on the very day which had been chosen to annihilate the Jews—cancelled that final solution. On that happy Purim day, an important Hebrew newspaper with a black border was published with a huge headline: "The people's sun has gone down." It had gone down on the camps where many had been annihilated, even members of the Young Guard.

The attempt had been made to disinherit the Ukrainians not

only from their country, but even from their history. Russia, which emerged on the world map with Ivan the Terrible at the end of the Middle Ages, had tried to lengthen its existence at the expense of stealing another people's history.

If, in history's next sharp turn, the Ukrainian people prove their maturity in relation to the Jews, the curse hanging over their land will turn into a blessing, as is customary for true penitents.

The Jewish "conspiracy"

I didn't know then, where and how the theory about the "conspiracy" had sprung up, but in the camps, it found fertile soil to grow in, particularly among the Russian nationalists. One Russian was honestly amazed how I, a Jew, didn't know anything about it. It couldn't be! I was only pretending innocence!

"But what kind of conspiracy is it?" I burst with stupid curiosity.

"How can it be? You don't know that the Jews control the world?"

"So what are we doing in the camps?"

"It's all to confuse the enemy."

"But why should the ruler confuse someone else?!"

"Oh, you don't understand anything. In the meantime, they secretly rule and accumulate power, in order to rule openly."

"And what about the six million victims?"

"Apparently, that was also a ruse in order to control the world."

"So where do the Jews rule?"

"Everywhere. Marx, Engels, Lenin, Stalin, Khrushchev, Brezhnev—they're all Jews. Even Nixon is a Jew."

"And Mao Zedong?" I smiled.

"Him too. The Jews even rule in Africa, only their skin color is black."

"And the pope?"

"All the popes are Jews. Just look at their pictures! Look at those noses!"

The Jewish "conspiracy"

"But noses like that are common in southern Europe!"

"Aha ... no! Here you can't make a mistake!"

"And Mao? How did he suddenly become a Jew?"

"Communism is a Jewish philosophy. And because of that, only a Jew can rule in a communist country. Besides, here in the *Literaturnaya Gazeta* [a literary magazine] it's written that the Israeli secret police informed him of the conspiracy against him!"

"But apparently you think that magazine is also Jewish."

"Of course! Moreover, even the Jews themselves admit it."

"Aren't you attributing supernatural powers to the Jews?"

"But the devil himself is behind them. He reveals himself to them. They rule through the offices of the freemasons, with its ninety degrees of certification. Only the Jews are on top, and below there are many others who do their will. The whole world is encircled."

"And how will this all end?"

"In a holocaust. When the Jews achieve their goal, everyone will rise against them. God will punish them."

And with those words and eyes burning with enthusiasm and tension, he began to prophesize in a wailing voice the horrific fate of the Jewish people. Hatred, as I was to understand shortly, was the backbone of his being—hatred, evil, revenge, and jealousy, the spirit of contradiction. He didn't live this way arbitrarily, he was always objecting to something or someone. To take away the idea of the enemy from him would mean taking away his life's breath. He would certainly commit suicide or drink himself to oblivion. Therefore, it was doubtful if he would be able to live anywhere outside Russia. He would return there, despite another period of imprisonment that awaited him.

In a normal country, among normal people, he would feel as if he were living in a vacuum; he would suffocate. Only in the atmosphere of the "conspiracy," the subversive connection, the atmosphere of life-long interrogation which could not be fled; only there would he feel that he was in his natural surroundings. Together with those who had arrested him, he unwittingly wanted these malicious waters to wash over and drown the entire universe. The world only appeared to him through the dark glasses of his soul. The evil concentrated in his personality had taken on a distinguishing code and image in one idea: Jew.

Actual Jews, for all their real activities and weaknesses, were connected to this very indirectly. The heated and sharply unrealistic theory, with its twisted logic, allowed any and all information to be integrated in the Procrustean bed of this theory. Communists behave in the same way when they interpret everything as absolute proof of their fabricated doctrine.

However, why had this brand of hatred in the world been turned against the Jews?

There were three reasons for it. First was the fact that the Jewish people saw themselves as a chosen people. From this arose the complex of "the slave who would be king," directed against the true chosen one. That was the hatred of Cain, the first big brother on earth. It wasn't for nothing that Soviet Russia called itself "big brother" in relation to the rest of the nationalities.

Second, the accepted custom in ruling Christianity to see the Jew as a creature worthy of contempt, the crucifier of Jesus, worthy to be a garbage can for emotions and society. When this garbage can rebelled against its status, it was perceived as if the world had gone topsy-turvy because of some monstrous "conspiracy."

And the last reason was the incomprehensible, mystical, unique destiny of the Jewish people. A destiny that clearly indicated a plan of great intent and deep enigma, difficult for an ordinary and superficial mind to grasp. Therefore, the theoreticians of the "conspiracy" debased, humiliated and monstrously distorted the great guiding hand from heaven to earth.

The intent of the conspiracy which existed in reality was that anti–Semitism should not only be convenient, but should pay off. Convenient because you could be portrayed as a warrior against worldwide evil without really being in danger. Moreover, the KGB saw this anti–Semitic "struggle" as something desirable and worthy, being directed objectively against all real opposition in the camp. As a prize of encouragement, Vagin, a follower of "The Protocols of the Elders of Zion," received an extra personal visit with relatives—something rare in the camp's younger circles. More than anything, the KGB feared meetings of prisoners with outside visitors who might uncover the camp's nakedness to the world's eyes. For that reason, they tried to prevent them. During all seven years of my incarceration, I only had one personal meeting with my mother.

The real conspiracy was indeed different. The KGB offered a poet—a political prisoner—an apartment in Moscow after her release, as well as a promise to publish her poems, an abundance of honors, and money. In exchange, only one thing was demanded of her: cooperation. Not only should she sing her poetry, but she should "sing" in the sense of inform. The "singing" poet was supposed to move about in opposition circles with the halo of a martyr hanging over her head. This particular poet absolutely refused. However, how many hadn't refused?

I participated in passing information from the Bolshevik prison to the free world. In many instances, it didn't succeed. So what? The worst facts of the regime's brutality were somehow put through a sieve. Who did this filtering? How was it done? In Moscow? In the West? En route? The secrecy of the chain made it very difficult to clarify things. In Moscow, stubborn rumors circulated that even certain Western newspapers and diplomats had received a second salary—from the KGB.

One of the Armenians who was in the camp had been an officer during World War II. Under Moscow's orders, Polish divisions had been formed and this Armenian had been sent as a commander. There had been no room for argument. Members of the Polish Army established by Moscow couldn't get along without a church. He was supposed to lead them there. They knelt, prayed, but he remained standing. Once a priest quietly approached him so that no one would hear and asked: "Why don't you kneel?" "I've been a communist for ten years already," the Armenian whispered. "And I've been a communist for twenty years," replied the priest. "Kneel!"

The church establishment swarmed with KGB agents who reported the secrets told them during confession. They distanced the people from faith due to the dissolute life they led. During the 1960s and 1970s, the communists massively infiltrated even the Western churches.

Nixon to you!

"Well, guys, the time has come to pack your suitcases!"

The guards were totally silent. They infrequently appeared on the camp grounds. They walked around as if asleep and barely harassed us. At that time, documents were arranged in the psychiatric hospitals with great urgency for the release of all those opponents of the regime who had suddenly been "cured." Some had already been released. The Soviet Union authorities expected an ultimatum from Nixon and were prepared to receive it. The bloc that had been created between the West and China was no joke! The Soviet Union was fearful of any possible union between the United States and China. A move that threatened to imprison it between a rock and a hard place. Were that to eventuate, the principal lever of Russian policy—blackmailing its opponent with threats of war—might become an empty threat.

Nixon preferred dealing with Russia. He came to Moscow in May 1972. His first announcement was that he didn't intend to interfere in the Soviet Union's internal affairs, because détente, and the development of a special relationship between them, was more important. The camps of terror had no place in the negotiations. This was exactly what the Bolsheviks wanted. The doors of the psychiatric hospitals slammed shut immediately, right in the faces of those preparing for release.

The guards lifted their heads up above the parapet of neutrality they adopted for expediency's sake during Nixon's visit, and returned to brutality.

Nearly half of the political prisoners were sent to the Urals. From the start, Nixon's additional visit brought a worsening of the oppression. We felt the effect of détente on our flesh. It was no wonder that after a short time it was also felt by those who had wanted to do business on our account—they felt it in Vietnam, in Angola, in the unheated apartments as a result of the oil embargo. We saw Watergate as punishment from heaven.

A new man

On the day Nixon left Moscow, for no reason, I was thrown into the punishment cells of the camp for six months.

A new man

That's how I was sent to the punishment cells. The guards forced the prisoners there to polish the frames of handcrafted table clocks. Initially, this was done "outside" the work cell. Afterward, "Lunokhod" (moon robot) Velmakin, deputy commander of the camp for government affairs, saw us and ordered to have us moved from the barbwired yard to the closed work cell.

The cell was moldy and wet. Tiny pieces of sawdust hung in the air and invaded our nostrils. A small fan slowly moved its blades inside the window opening, changing nothing in the cell. Appearances were improved if nothing more: there was "ventilation." There was no sense asking to see a doctor.

The wife of the camp commander, Osov, was a short, stout woman with the legs of an elephant, and constantly furious. She ran the medical department. She hated me with a burning passion, and would have eaten me alive. I didn't know why. Nikolai, my cellmate, and I began a strike. We preferred to be thrown into solitary, watching the summer grass turn yellow and brown beyond the window woven with alarm wires as thin as a spider's threads, so that we would no longer be forced to work in that moldy, dusty room.

In 1972, God didn't bless the Bolsheviks with rain. America, as usual, got them out of the mud, and supplied them with bread. A friend in need! Therefore, it was possible to continue the routine of oppression despite the total failure of the communist economy. "Lunokhod" would enter our solitary cells, but we didn't even get up. Velmakin became sad and stopped visiting us. However, so that in the future we wouldn't be able to lie down with our backs to the administration, his slaves were ordered to smash the wooden planks. A Nazi-capo, Zvegorodny, one of the prominent collaborators with

The Guards Spoke Russian

the Germans in Kharkhov, now work manager in the camp, and a veteran "benefactor," was the one who conducted the "improvements" in the punishment cells to make them better suited for torturing prisoners.

He made heroic efforts, trying with all his might; his orders rang out under the low ceilings of the small prison. For prisoners, making disciplinary implements to assist in punitive measures was considered a contemptible deed. However, in the camp where the *polizei* chorus sang on the club stage "the party is our leader" (which party—the Nazi or the Communist one?), those who felt shame and those who had a conscience weren't particularly numerous.

The Soviet empire was characterized by its aspiration to first of all erode the individual's moral foundation—otherwise, he couldn't be a perfect cog in the machine. The hangman demanded that his victims, even under torture, sing psalms of praise to the regime. He was more sensitive to any spark of honesty than he was to bullets. Furthermore, the songs of praise, as false as they were, were necessary for the especially cynical hangman in order to lie to everyone around him. Generally, there was enough of an interested audience, attracted like a magnet to this nauseating drama. Could it be that this was due to the dimensions of the tragicomedy, in which 300 million actors appeared all at once as clowns on this tumultuous stage, the vastest in human history? An individual whose sense of shame had been eroded would do everything for his own benefit or out of fear. For that reason the main purpose of the regime was to push him toward this theater, to destroy and atrophy his soul. The perfect "new man" was the one who could no longer blush.

Unfortunately, there were also young people under Zvegorodny's command. One of them sang, told jokes about guards, and offered to pour more water on the fresh cement. The irony of fate was that he was the one who became the first to enter the new solitary confinement for two days. However, even this didn't wise him up. During those two days, he tried to make as many frames as he could, so that afterward they would raise the quota for all those who followed him in the punishment cells. In exchange, the guards brought him bread.

The big transfer from Mordovia to the Urals

Railroad tracks ran next to the fence of Camp 19, near the huge iron gate and the watchtowers. One of their sidetracks entered the camp in order to bring in railroad cars, squeaking from too much weight, loaded with tree trunks, to then unload well-wrapped, finished product from them.

Now, an entire train of Stolypin* cars stood in front of the camp and swallowed up a mass of prisoners within its dark innards. We were only allowed to be happy and enjoy the blazing, sun-filled sky for a short time as we stood and awaited our turn, even though as prisoners from the punishment cells, we were loaded on last.

The watchmen carried on and shouted, completely undressed us and searched. They even saw something very suspicious in our nakedness and were ready to penetrate our skin. Crude shouts, cursing, wildly enraged glances, and malicious hatred, with weapons drawn and aimed for action. Some of the cages in the car were purposely left empty, and we were squeezed into what remained, after a thorough search.

They even took the keys to the suitcases (were they weapons too?). I didn't get mine back. Apparently, they eventually threw them out. There was nowhere to sit. The heat was insufferable, but the watchmen purposely didn't open windows. People like that shot into protesting crowds, trampled demonstrating members of their own people with tanks in Novocherkassk in 1962, when hungry workers, their wives and children went out into the streets to demand bread. Those who remained alive, whose intestines and hair hadn't been caught in the tanks' chains, had been sent in large numbers to the camps completely cut off from the outside world, denied the right

---

*Stolypin—minister and prime minister in tsarist Russia at the beginning of the 20th century. His reforms also brought reform in the area of punishment. The prison cars in Russia are still today called "Stolypin cars."

The Guards Spoke Russian

Prisoners' walk.

to write letters. It is said, even today, when these lines are being written, that they still are suffering somewhere on the banks of the Pechora. However, there were exceptions. Such as the local garrison commander who shot himself because he didn't want his lips to pronounce the terrible order to his soldiers. It sometimes happened that the watchtower guards committed suicide when they couldn't take it any longer.

Every hour, the watchmen broke into our packed cage, stepped on the boards with their dirty boots, felt around, and searched for something with a flashlight. They set upon us, shoved us, and counted heads.

Days and nights, and more nights and days, we crawled along the Russian plains. We intentionally detoured around the large stations in order to preserve the secrecy of the journey. The train stopped at dead-end side tracks so that no one would see us. The cars were traveling northward carrying nearly half of Mordovia's prisoners from the political camps, Camp 3, 17, and 19. There was no room for sleeping. We tried to lie on the floor because we couldn't manage on the planks which were crowded beyond capacity. Right away we heard the crude shouts, the swearing:

"Get up! It's forbidden! Quickly! Quickly! Fuck you!"

"So where shall we sleep?"

"Wherever you want! You're not on vacation, sons of…! Bloody rebels! Damn you…!"

There was an atmosphere of civil war, as if it would never end.

A very sick old man, Orlovitch, was in the cage with us. He had a good heart and was quiet, like many Byelorussians. He was completely sunk into his large, grey-streaked beard, and only looked around with a forlorn glance. It was difficult to obtain permission to go to the bathroom, and when finally people were taken out, one by one, they left the door open, and a soldier stood over us shouting wildly: "Quickly, quickly! What, are you settling down?! Quickly, motherfuckers!"

Orlovitch had bleeding of the large intestine. The long imprisonment had disrupted his digestive system function. Even under regular conditions, it was hard for him to move his bowels, and in the presence of another person, he suffered from cramps. He had not had a bowel movement for several days. He was almost certain he would die and that he wouldn't reach the destination. He couldn't even manage to urinate. For those two days, we pleaded with the watchmen to let the old man sit quietly in the bathroom, not to drive him out, to close the door. After all, where could this miserable, barely living being escape to through the iron walls? Finally, we somehow managed to persuade the red epaulets. Orlovitch was saved.

We were traveling parallel to the Volga River. The kingdom of the Khazars, the great Jewish state, had been here in the distant past.

The iron railroad car heated up under the sun's rays. It was insufferably suffocating, and even the soldiers on guard, who weren't sitting in the crammed cages but were walking along the corridor next to them, couldn't stand it any longer. They half opened the sealed windows, and the prisoners looked out from the dark cages facing the corridor of the car, fascinated by the crack from which they glimpsed the great world. Apparently, that's how a blind person looks when he suddenly regains his sight.

A clear day. Steep hills all around. Geologists with their instruments, and among them, a woman in pants, all sat on a carpet of tangled grass... The pictures passed by quickly; scenery, bathing beaches full of people tanning, again women... And meanwhile, I remembered a story from the camp, a story of a Soviet Oedipus. One of the prisoners was caught having sexual relations with his mother who had come to visit him. "Who else but me would have pity on him...?" the mother cried under interrogation.

The open window saved us a bit from suffocation.

In other cars, where the guarding was even more offensive, prisoners reached such despair that they coordinated rocking the car from side to side. They preferred a quick death. The watchmen were indeed alarmed by the possibility that the car would turn over. Only then did they withdraw. The windows were opened, earning the prisoners several breaths of air.

We received water only after pleas and struggle. They were saving it, guarding every drop. The watchmen didn't even consider letting us use it for washing. For all the days of travel, the prisoners washed only in their own sweat in the crowded and sweltering cages. The heat and suffocation were so strong that sweat poured over the people like rain. The skin on our fingers shrunk as if after repeated washing. Heart attacks, fainting, and one instance of death along the route—with no relief and no assistance.

Already the hills and peaks of the Ural Mountains appeared, covered with the fir trees typical of the taiga, dark and threatening expanses. Remote and neglected settlements; deformed, ugly human figures; the fires of hell from huge furnaces—strong, sulfurous and choking smoke crawled over the land fluttering in the wind; lop-sided wooden houses blackened with age, and frequently inhabited by people together with their animals. No orchards, no flowers, no beautiful tended vegetable gardens like those surrounding the clean, white houses of the Ukraine. Everything was desolate, filthy, bare and dark; miserable, neglected and skimpy fields covered with yellow stubs of blighted wheat, as if taken from pharaoh's dream. Everything created a sorrowful atmosphere of death. This dark, black, severed land was made for animals and not humans. Many drunks tottered about or lay in the roadways. Here they were—the saviors of humanity! From the window, we saw huge fires several times. The dryness was terrible. In one of the settlements, the coals that remained from the burnt houses were still hissing, in another the flames had only begun to rise.

For some reason, I remembered Sacko Torosian, the political prisoner from Armenia. He had come once to "Political Studies" in Camp 19. Most of the prisoners boycotted it, but he had come with defiant intent and asked the officer how to interpret the right of the Armenian people for self-determination. Armenia was the most ancient and strongest of all the occupied countries in the empire. This ancient people possessed a great culture. After the class, "Hitler," the criminal prisoner whose real name was Kornikov, began to attack Torosian.

"You're not a nation, you're profiteers," he goaded Torosian. "You only know how to trade in your fruit and profit by Russia's poverty!"

"Who's to blame that you're poor," Sacko protested. "Who stops you from bringing your potatoes to Yerevan [the capital of Armenia]?

The Guards Spoke Russian

There are no potatoes in Armenia. Potatoes are more expensive there than Armenian fruit in Russia! Bring them, sell them, everyone will thank you! But no, you need to drink and get drunk, to destroy and steal, and when the food is finished and there's nothing to eat, you push your way into the land of ours which you haven't yet completely destroyed."

"Hitler" began a quarrel, fell upon Sacko with a drawn knife in front of the entire barrack, but no one punished him. Only Sacko alone managed to overcome him, to throw the knife aside, and to "rumple" his ribs a bit. Now, in the neighboring cage, there was one of the most important members of the band of thugs later organized in the Urals. Together with "Hitler," they engaged in terror there upon the political prisoners. You could hear how he was angrily arguing with Simchitch, one of the fighters for Ukrainian independence, about the "Jewish conspiracy."

"What, are those the Jews who won't give you water to drink? That nonsense doesn't work on anyone anymore," Simchitch's voice was heard to say.

Suddenly the guarding soldiers stopped next to our cage. They peered attentively into the darkness and called my name. They held a bunch of papers in their hands. What was happening?

"Get your things ready!"*

"Where to? We're on a moving train!"

They led me through the swaying cars into a small cage where there were already two young men from Camp 17. It turned out that this entire car was full of prisoners from Camp 17. If this was the case, I would be sitting in the Urals together with them. Where was Shimon? At the other end of the car. We called out to each other in Yiddish. Joseph Mendelevich was also in the cage with Shimon. God willing, we would become acquainted.

The train stopped. One by one, the prisoners were removed. I was among the last ones. The entire area of the station was surrounded

---

*"Your things" – in Russia there was an absolute prohibition on announcing to a prisoner the destination he was being transported to. They only used to inform him to leave "with his things," or "without his things." "With his things" meant being transferred somewhere. "Without his things" usually meant taking a prisoner to be interrogated.

The big transfer from Mordovia to the Urals

by red epaulets, with weapons cocked and German Shepherd dogs. The prisoners gathered en masse. There wasn't enough room for this many prisoners in the "crows."* So they piled everyone into open trucks, guarded by machine guns. Several dozen, me among them, were crammed into each "crow." I didn't know anyone. They were all from other camps. I sat in this iron box, squeezed in on all sides.

The "crow" madly raced on the horrid Ural roadways, skipping from pothole to pothole, shaking up our intestines. It seemed as if this pathway of hell would never end; one curve after another. One great upheaval after another; a burst of bumps and bruises. We arrived at the camp gate, barely alive. The "crow" remained sealed shut. The prisoners began to pound with their fists on the burning hot iron, hot from the summer sun. There was no response. A half hour later, a soldier appeared.

"What's the matter?"

"We're stifling ... the heat ... we need the bathroom ... water..."

"Wait!"

"I need the bathroom! I can't bear it anymore! Let me out!"

"Go in your pants!" laughed the soldier, pleased with his joke.

The stifling heat continued. We were being roasted in an iron cage under the sun's beating rays. Pounding, shouting, cursing, fainting, groaning.

I sat without moving. I didn't want to waste my strength and give the hangmen superfluous pleasure. The others were simply finished. Those who still had some strength began to sway the "crow" from side to side so that it would turn over with all of us in it. Anyway, we were anticipating a similar end. One of the prisoners tried to cut his veins and I restrained him.

When the doors were finally opened after several hours, I wobbled out. My clothes could have been wrung out; my head was empty of thought. Only deep inhalations and exhalations, opening my mouth like a fish.

Shimon fell upon me in the camp, almost suffocating me with his hugs. I barely got to the pump and drank. I drank the

---

*A nickname for the prisoner transport trucks.

swamp-smelling water from my palm, and it seemed to me that it was the best-tasting water in the world.

In the miserable bathhouse, brimming with people, I hugged Oleg and made the acquaintance of several others. Filthy tubs, lines next to the faucet, sewage water on the floor. Somehow we bathed. Afterward we sat down on the grass and began to revive. However, we were only given a few days to remain among friends. All the prisoners, one by one, were called to headquarters where the new administration was sitting. When I was brought in, the KGB supervisor over the political prisoner camps, Afanasov, shouted:

"He hasn't completed his term in the punishment cells! He has to complete it!"

None of those who had traveled with me in the "crow" had completed his incarceration in the punishment cells, but he didn't mention that. Afterward, it became clear why they hadn't taken me to Camp 35 with the rest of the prisoners from Camp 19. The punishment cells in Camp 35 still weren't ready. I was the only one transferred from Camp 19 in Mordovia to Camp 36 in the Urals. I was the only one of all the many who hadn't completed their time in the cells and, immediately upon my arrival at Camp 36, I was thrown into the punishment cells until I had served my time there. In this context, I remembered a conversation between two criminal prisoners with whom I had been in prison. One of them said to his companion:

"It says on your forehead 'Keep plowing!' and on the back of your neck, the rest says 'with no vacation days!'"

What was written on my forehead? Apparently it said "set apart"—as well as on the forehead of my people.

There were prisoners who wrote their thoughts on their foreheads in the camps known for their severe regimes. For example, one of the typical tattoos was: "Slave of the Party." Skin was removed from their forehead because of things like that, so that a scar might run from temple to temple between hairline and eyebrows. They were also given additional periods of imprisonment. Some of them were even sentenced to death. They were executed because of a few words of truth and these death sentences continued into the early 1970s.

The ship of fools

When I was taken out for a half hour walk in the punishment cell yard, the sky was covered with smoke. The horizon was blurred, forests, houses, burning peat. The sky sent fire down upon Cain's earth.

The ship of fools

Several days later, the quiet in my solitary cell was shaken by the shouts of a prisoner who had been put in the adjacent solitary cell. It turned out that my neighbor was rather temperamental and restless, day and night. He was, as he presented himself in jest, "Vladimir de Krasniak, serf of the Kremlin, a white slave in the land of the Soviets."

Krasniak was a criminal prisoner. He was well known throughout the prison. Once, after having been injected with some substance, and having been taken from the clinic on a stretcher, a sure sign of death, in spite of this, his spirit had not fallen. "The experiment didn't succeed! The victim is alive!" His cry from the stretcher was heard all over the camp.

He was again placed in solitary, I understood, because of friction with the camps' therapists. First of all, he shattered his small glass window and began to give speeches through the bars in the direction of the settlement of "free people" adjoining the camp.

"The victim is in the death ward! Come, communists, drink his blood! Trample his body with your feet; step on your resurrected Lenin, too!"

"Krasniak, what Lenin are you talking about?" the guards who looked through the peephole asked with interest.

"Here he is!" called Krasniak, turning to the door and opening his fly. "Here he is! Can you see? Bald with a little beard! Look, look, he's being resurrected!"

"Ah, you, so and so!" and the guards turned away from the door choking with both laughter and annoyance.

Krasniak somewhere had seen a reproduction of Pieter Brueghel's

The Guards Spoke Russian

painting *The Ship of Fools*. It had been etched in his sensitive awareness, and now he shouted in a thundering voice, heard in all the cells, his routine message: "To the Kremlin ship of fools, to the captain Brezhnev. Change your sailing direction, Leonid!" and so on and so forth.

And again, Krasniak "orated," as he called it, with all the force in his lungs. He roared and pounded with his boots on the wooden board. "Communists to the zoo! Comsomols [members of the communist youth] to the moon! Communists, comsomols, patriots—subhumans!"

Gradually, his slogans, "broadcast" in the direction of the guards' "settlement," stirred around in my brain and wouldn't leave me alone. However, apparently this wasn't only happening in my brain. Sometime afterward, Brezhnev, the possessor of the "eyebrow sails," in one of his fateful speeches, used one of Krasniak's colorful descriptions: "Our ship," the leader called, with his heavy tongue breaking the slight sighing of the anti–Soviet waves, "Our ship is sailing on its course. The wind of history fills our sails!" The plagiarism was clear, and Krasniak didn't forgive such things.

Krasniak was also fascinated by unidentified flying objects, by mysterious flying saucers. He used them in his next complex slogan: "Hooray for Katka's underwear [Catherine Furtseva, the then Soviet Minister of Cultural Affairs] and for the circus pole with the twirling saucers above Lenin's bald head! Hooray! Long live the saucers dancing over the Kremlin ship of fools!"

Grigoriev liked the slogan about Katka. He was a deserter in the neighboring cell. Imitating Krasniak, he also shattered the window and began to scream out the slogans he heard.

"Hey, you, stop it!" Krasniak angrily said. "I've been thinking up that slogan for three years! Yell your own slogans!" Krasniak, full of renewed strength, yelled out: "A c--- in the throat of Kotov (the commander of Camp 36), commander of the death camp!"

"A c--- in the throat of your Brezhnev!"

Krasniak named his slop bucket "Katka Furtseva."

In the meantime, the solitary confinement cells were filling up. More and more people received additional prison sentences, the "material" accumulated, and several were moved for several months to the punishment cells. Thus, my solitude ended. During my talks in the barred and barbed wire yard, I would occasionally merit Vladimir "De" Krasniak's company. Grigoriev shared the cell with me. He was a pale, thin youth, and he was in a state of constant shock due to the terror of the camps.

Everything was mixed up for him: the idea of Christian asceticism, criminal slang, and politics. He was half Russian and half Ukrainian. His parents had divorced, and this added more instability and internal contradictions. As a result of all this, he didn't know how to shut his mouth. He talked incessantly about everything, while his blue eyes protruded in an amusing manner and he wrinkled his white forehead. However, the most sensitive subject for him was sex. On this subject the innocence of Christian theory was diluted by the corruption of a boy of the streets.

With a frustrated, internal storminess, he told about where, how, and with whom some anonymous person had sexual relations. I remember, for example, stories about how the girls of his school became pregnant. One of them, during class time at school and while sitting at a desk in the rear, opened the buttons on her boyfriend's pants. Another, who was 12 years old when she began to feel sexual desires, came to an older boy she knew, to seemingly ask to borrow a reading book. When he later approached her with the requested book in his hand, he was amazed to see her in her birthday suit and ready for anything…

At that time, I had a nightmare. It was as if I wasn't sleeping, but was lying in my cell. I looked at the window and against the background of the bars, somehow one of my cellmates was lying down within the double frame, perhaps sleeping, perhaps dead, with his body leaning a bit on its side, and his eyes shut. I turned around and saw him lying on the plank next to me! It was frightening—my cellmate sleeping next to me. At the same moment, his double in the window woke up, rose slightly and looked at me with the malicious grin of a murderer. I woke up in a cold sweat. Only afterward, in another place and another situation, I understood. This was a sign of things to come. Years later, we met in Vladimir Prison and then I understood the warning.

During the hours of the day, Major Feyodorov and Captains

The Guards Spoke Russian

Makhnutin and Rotenko abused us, looked for and found a million reasons and excuses to set upon us. However, we had no rest at night either. Our small window nearly joined the sealed camp wall, above which stood a machine gunner in a watchtower. In the middle of the night, an awful, inhuman shout would wake us up: "Stand, who goes there!!!"

You could have a heart attack after one of those "stands!" The guard shouted so much, as if burning with the desire to prove how much effort he put into serving the homeland, even though it was only a change of the guard. During the day, machine gun fire beyond the fence, the shrieking yelps of the German shepherd dogs, the harsh shouts of the supervisors, the footsteps of the marchers, loud salutes by the soldiers on watch: "Greetings of well-being, comrade commander!"

It seemed as if a chorus of trained dogs answered them on cue: Bow-wow-wow-wow-wow!

With the coming of the cold season, Major Feyodorov made sure of one thing—that all the cells with walls covered in water and ice be completely occupied. He used to leave the camp's territory in order to hunt down prisoners. Otherwise, he would come to the prison in order to enjoy a tough game of cat with the mice he had hunted. When we went out for a walk, we clearly heard how the red epaulets were being trained on the other side of the fence.

One of the regular guests in the punishment cells was Major Kiselyov, an old anti–Semite, who wrote such garbled reports that the prisoners used to quote them to each other as an example of stupidity.

"So, how do we feel?" he would ask us with a disparaging hypocrisy as we walked in the closed cage.

"We're having an argument. There's something we can't totally understand!"

"So, what is it?"

"The communists say that they are descended from the monkey and we believe them. We can assume that they know their origin. However, exactly what kind of monkey? A gorilla or a macaque?"

Kiselyov was terribly insulted. Despite being a communist at the time of his service as major in the camp police, rumors went around that he secretly attended church to pray for his sins abundantly accumulated even from the days of Beria, Stalin's infamous interior minister. However, that didn't prevent him from continuing to sin.

"I asked Dr. Kotova, the wife of the camp commander, to take me as a dog!" Krasniak related his routine wisecrack. "I committed myself to sit chained up and to bark all night. I'm prepared to live in a doghouse, and the main thing is to be fed like a dog. But, she was afraid that I would eat her and her children!"

"Hey, hey, what wishes! A dog has to be given meat, or at least bones!"

"Yes, gentlemen, we are always demanding human rights, but if only we merited the rights of animals! Indeed, the communists recognize man as a social animal. An animal needs a mat under him—and there's no need for us to have one in solitary! The owner doesn't starve his dog—and we are starved! A dog has a warm doghouse and they throw us practically naked on cold cement! In this situation, we should be complaining to the Humane Society! We're not considered humans, so at least let them recognize us as animals! They'd be tried in court for such treatment to animals!" That's how the prisoners spoke to each other, improvising following Krasniak's offer to be a dog.

The commander of the camp's medical department, lame Petrov, used to visit the punishment cells and ask strange questions: "So, how are you getting along with each other here? What are you busy with? Don't you fight? What are you reading?"

"Homer."

"Homer? But what exactly? Novels, short stories?"

"Comedies, doctor…"

Once we were walking in our wired cage when Dr. Petrov marched through the prison to the camp.

"Oh, Dash-Dash is coming here Dash-Dash!" Krasniak greeted him when he arrived. Without noticing us, Petrov limped with his cane to the punishment cell's outer corner, opened the fly on his pants and in front of everyone, serenely urinated. The bathroom was only a few paces away, but that didn't embarrass this smart man.

"And Doctor Krauzer took out the Mauser..."; Krasniak accompanied the deed with rhymed commentary from a melody by some Odessan smart alecks.

It was good that lately they had begun to speak not only about the reasons for the incarcerations, but also about the conditions. The Bolsheviks, of course, attempted to rely on the maximum of what a prisoner could obtain if he collaborated with his torturers in every sense. It was now time to force them to speak about the guaranteed minimum for every situation and in every instance, even for a prisoner who didn't place himself on the path to "re-education"—if, for example, he had refused to participate in the slave labor that contributed to the criminal system. The minimum was: Zero meetings (total isolation). Zero letters (everything was confiscated by the censors, or simply stolen). No medical assistance (or worse—intentional harm to health with appropriate instruments). A system of humiliation and abuse. Prevention of the basic conditions for a routine existence. Torture by means of hunger and cold. KGB incitement and provocation.

Adding this mixture to the prison terms (twenty five years, for example), and only an imagination like Dante's was able to grasp the essential meaning of this minimum.

Back to the wire

From the punishment cells, I returned drained and completely exhausted to the camp.

My face was yellowish-white, as white as the snow flurrying in the evening in the camps' flashlights. My legs hurt a great deal in the first days from just normal walking. In my mind, I again heard Krasniak's slogans, which I had heard daily for months. The odor of the slop bucket, the most loathsome of everything I knew, still pursued me. It seemed that at some point, someone had not controlled himself and had defecated in the bucket and no one had emptied it. They moved the bucket to our cell in its advanced state of rottenness. When Grigoriev lifted the lid, those of us in the cell nearly fainted from the disgusting stench. A slop bucket never emits fragrant perfumes, but this was something extraordinary even for this kind of vessel. At times, I thought it would be better to die rather than breathe in this insufferable stench again.

During my absence, the camp had observed the "Day of the Red Terror" for the first time. Those of us in the cells only went on a hunger strike on that day, and we didn't see the ceremony. On September 5, 1918, immediately following the beginning of the Red Terror, Lenin had ordered the establishment of the first concentration camps, which were then augmented in Stalin's time. Hitler had someone to learn from…

It was September 5, 1972. The previous evening, the prisoners had gathered secretly in one of the unfinished buildings. There was a symbolic burial mound surrounded by barbed wire in the middle. Representatives of all the communities, each one in turn, read prayers in memory of the tortured. Platonov prayed at length. The Ukrainians knelt and said "May God remember our tortured to death brothers' souls."

Joseph Mendelevitch said a hurried and melodic kaddish. There were also Armenians, representatives of the Baltic peoples, Muslims from the Caucasus who prayed in Arabic. A large candle was placed on the burial mound by each community and the candles illumined the awful darkness. Afterward, each person, whose relatives had been killed by the communists, placed a small candle in memory of each of them. There were many candles.

"Chekist Day" (the day for the workers in the secret police, the KGB—such a holiday existed in the Soviet Union) was marked by the day's "celebrants" with mass searches. The storeroom for possessions was abruptly closed. The guards and the Chekists summoned the prisoners individually, demanded the transfer of their possessions to another place, and performed the most thorough search. They confiscated a number of writings from Simas Kudirka (they particularly devoted attention to hunting down papers). A Lithuanian Chekist began to rebuke Kudirka, also a Lithwanian. Simas, who always spoke the whole truth without being a smart aleck, got annoyed and called him a traitor and collaborator. They sent Simas to the punishment cells. Possessions that hadn't been identified by the prisoners were confiscated. Among Joseph Mendelevitch's possessions, they found a small wooden menorah, his own handiwork, and they took it and threw it in the trash. A forbidden object! In the next search following the menorah, they confiscated a Jewish bible which had been smuggled into the camp.

A third of the camp grounds was fenced in additional barbed wire, and beyond it was the swamp. In the summer, a vapor of dampness and rot rose from it. For those sick with tuberculosis, more than just a few, this was like sticking a knife in their throat. When the summer arrived, there was no escape from the brigades of mosquitoes and other blood-sucking, flying insects that covered the sky like clouds. The Mordovian blood-suckers looked insignificant to us now in comparison to these. We heard of instances in which an especially problematic prisoner would be undressed by the guards and bound to a tree on the other side of the fence. According to plan, he would be immediately engulfed by a cloud of mosquitoes and would slowly die from numerous bites.

The ridge of the Urals, parallel to the longitude lines, served as a track for the strong winds, steering them from the north or south. With each slight directional change of the wind, this phenomenon created severe changes in temperature and humidity. It was hot and you were wearing a shirt, when suddenly it became unbearably cold, even if you were wearing a pea coat! The barometric pressure also jumped with huge fluctuations. This caused much suffering for those with high blood pressure.

Minus 54° Centigrade

The winter came accompanied by cold that was so harsh and wild that it seemed as if everything had fallen apart. The cold pierced the

Minus 54° Centigrade

air like sharp needles. Lungs contracted from the force of the cold. Most of the political prisoners were from the southern climes or the Baltic seacoast. The water froze in the water tank. Cold penetrated the barrack and the factory. Major Feyodorov immediately began a campaign of confiscating "unnecessary" clothing. At the height of the cold, everything was removed other than the miserable prison uniforms and people were forced to part from their improvised undershirts.

Meanwhile, new prisoners arrived at the camp. Olexa Reznikov was big and strong, blue-eyed and had a moustache the color of ripe wheat. He was quiet and very cautious. Sometimes it appeared that he was apathetic. As a matter of fact, he was a talented Ukrainian poet, with a deep knowledge of his nation's language, and very sensitive to words and their power. Initially, he was sent to the camp because of a banner against "the fascist tyranny of the party." He was still far from nationalist ideals then, but during his period of imprisonment, his eyes were opened. After his release, he lived in Odessa. He began to develop as an artist there and his creative personality reached full maturation and expression there. In a city where no word of Ukrainian was heard, a unique Ukrainian poet was an unusual phenomenon. He was arrested a second time for the crime of distributing something from the "Samizdat,"* as it were, although there was no evidence of this "terrible" crime.

During the trial, the prosecutor asked one of the witnesses with severity: "And you warned the accused to stop engaging in this activity?!"

"Yes, yes," the witness trembled. "I warned him: shave your moustache, don't speak Ukrainian, otherwise the authorities will get after you!"

Oles Sergeyenko wasn't even born in Ukraine, but in exile, in the city of Tambov, where the police tried by every means to force his family of exiles to register as Russians. They vehemently refused.

"Oh ho, damned nationalists!" the policewoman shrieked at them with helpless anger.

---

*"Samizdat"—"independent publication"—a folk publication of works by simple means such as a printing press.

The Guards Spoke Russian

Body searching.

Minus 54° Centigrade

The family continued to preserve its language, its way of life, and its unique culture in its Russian surroundings. At the first opportunity, they returned to Kiev. While he had still been a child, Oles dreamed that he finally heard his mother tongue in the city streets. In Kiev, bitter disappointment awaited him. Many of his relatives had died in the camps, in exile, and Siberia was carpeted with their bones. Now, he too was there, on the Siberian border.

Spring approached. The snow began to thaw. The sound of dripping icicles was heard. Purim came. The guard was reinforced. They arrested all the Jews, searched them, followed them, and often entered the barracks. We were forced to gather for the meager festival meal in two groups, each group in its barrack. Afterward, we all gathered outside in the evening cold. Joseph Mendelevitch invoked images and described in words the Purim-spiel suited to our times that was being presented in those days in Russian Jewish circles.

We rolled over in laughter and "Hamans," in their red epaulets, circled around us. Every so often, curious prisoners approached us. We didn't understand how the guards had sniffed us out and found out about Purim. They behaved as if the camp had been preparing a rebellion.

Afterward, when I was no longer in the Urals, the Christians decided to celebrate their Easter; the weather even permitted them to organize a modest "picnic." The guards didn't succeed in dispersing the Christians. They were the majority and didn't give in to threats. Then, the nearby sewage pump began to operate, and ruined the feast with its stench.

The police turned crueler toward us. We all felt that something was changing on the outside. They spoke about a real spiritual rebellion at the Ukrainian writers' conference. Even the honorable chairman himself, Malishko, declared publicly that the idea to assimilate the Ukrainian people was a fascistic idea. A short time later, Malishko died under mysterious circumstances. In Stalin's torture chambers, Ukrainian authors had lost numbers many times greater than on the fronts of World War II. One by one they had been uprooted and were replaced by collaborators who were loyal to the regime. In spite of this, rebellion ripened among them.

The kidnapped spring

Complaint writing became the fashion in the camp. Although we knew that there was no benefit to it, it caused inconvenience to the guards who were supposed to formulate a formal response, even if it was the biggest lie, for the "supervising" attorney's office.

Therefore, the guards viewed each complaint as an act of protest. They began to take revenge. I wrote a complaint about the water which was impossible to properly wash with. The water left a dark and slippery crust on the sink, and its odor was like that of a swamp. Our clothes, washed in the bathhouse, had rusty stains left by the water that didn't come off. There were rumors that added that the water was also radioactive because there were uranium mines nearby. Camp commander Kotov ordered me to present myself to discuss the complaint.

There had been time upon our arrival at the camp when the administration used to be so stupid and unpredictable that prisoners were punished for using words such as "nuance," or penitentiary system in their complaints, because the commanders thought they were coarse expressions. Even their "higher" judicial education didn't help them absorb nuances such as those.

Now, Kotov, who had become "cultured" in the meantime, simply proposed not to send the complaints but to take them back. I refused. (As an aside, different commissions came several times later on, inspected the state of the water, and reached the conclusion that it wasn't fit to be used—and everything remained as it had been.)

"So, that's it? You refuse?" Kotov significantly asked again. He called Rak, the guard officer who specialized in dirty deeds.

"Knock that *yarmulke* off his head!" Kotov thundered his order at Rak and pointed at me with an artificial, theatrical gesture.

Rak reached out his arm and instinctively I covered my head with my hands.

"Defiance! To solitary!" shrieked Kotov.

They dragged me to solitary. When the ten days of official

punishment had ended, they added another ten. They meant to keep it up until the "final victory."

However, representatives of our organized community approached the KGB representative in the camp, declaring that if my stay in solitary was again lengthened, they would do something that had never been heard of before. The solidarity helped. The KGB withdrew. Instead of again lengthening my stay in solitary, they decided to send me to Vladimir Prison (the infamous "Vladimirsky Central").

While I was in solitary, the guard, Makhnutin, was excelling in searches accompanied by stripping off the prisoner's clothing until naked. His fellow specialist, Rotenko, wouldn't take me to the storeroom in the evening, as was customarily done with those sitting in solitary to select one of the sleeping planks. Nevertheless, he wasn't lazy and he brought me the plank with his own hands. This was the narrowest plank that could be found, made only out of three narrow boards with huge gaps between them.

Occasionally, Sharikov, the camp administration officer, arrived. He surprisingly was reminiscent of Mikhail Bulgakov's character, whose name was the same. Bulgakov's Sharikov was created by a brilliant surgeon out of a street mutt, and, after surgery, he retained all of a dog's habits, despite his human form. Our Sharikov was the usual tattooed criminal sort. He specialized in provocation. He used to invite prisoners to his room and wildly shout threats at them, abuse them, and egg them on to react. I refused to talk to him. After several wild shouts, he was perplexed by the fact that I showed no reaction. Fatigued, he ordered the guards to remove me from his room.

All of a sudden, without being told where they were taking me or why, I was taken straight from solitary to the camp's internal court, which judged prisoners for disciplinary misdemeanors. It went this way. "Last name, first name, father's name?" a cross-eyed woman who sat at a desk in the center of the "triumvirate," directed at me as soon as I was brought into the room.

"I'm a Jew and I only speak Hebrew," I answered in my people's tongue which they didn't understand. The judge crossed her eyes even more. She was stunned and didn't know what to do. However, the police whispered to her, seated me in the corner and directed the comedy without paying attention to me. Why should they translate when the whole business was only a formality? After all, the KGB had already made their decision.

They sentenced me to three years in jail for keeping Jewish customs. It was as if I was non-existent for the lady judges. They looked at the wall behind me as if I was transparent. It was only paperwork that had to be arranged in the fairest and most pleasing manner, according to the instructions received from the KGB. In the prosecution's writ, it said: "He sees himself as a prisoner-of-war." They included that, according to Makhnutin's reports, after he once led me to say something honestly, in spite of everything. Indeed, that was his specialty—"honesty."

After some rest in a lone cell, a "normal" camp food ration, and relative quiet from the guards—thanks to the protests of my group—the transfer to Vladimir Prison awaited me. Already sitting in the neighboring isolation cell were Simas Kudirka, Oles Sergeyenko, and Alex Safronov, a deserter with dramatic tendencies and a general air of amusement. Sounds of laughter were frequently heard. There are people who know how to laugh anywhere.

A white cockroach

They led me to the watch room situated between two sealed fences that separated the camp from the outside world. In spite of that, the group could tell something (maybe they saw through one of the cracks?) of what was going on. Voices saying good-bye wafted over the high fence: "We'll meet in Jerusalem!" my Jewish brothers yelled.

"A speedy release!" others wished me.

I answered their wishes in a loud voice, in the same manner. The escorting guard, knowing that it was already impossible to send me back to solitary (because I was already leaving), reacted with moderation.

A white cockroach

The terrible camp gates, the guard post, the exit, machine gunners with their weapons cocked. "The crow," the "cup" (a tiny iron cell, isolated, attached to the prisoners' truck). I was again jostled and knocked around like a fly on a glass window, on Russia's insufferably bumpy roads. It seemed that right away my guts were emptied, my internal organs were torn apart, and my bones were broken. After this hell, an almost eternal one—the truck stopped. Guards' voices were heard as though through cotton wool. They sat peacefully on their soft seats, talking about this and that.

"Yes, the war will begin with China and they'll send us there," said one of the soldiers fearfully.

"That's not like transporting prisoners," the second agreed with him.

I remembered my roommate's conversations with his drinking buddies in the room I had lived in before my arrest, when they absorbed the fact that because they had totally failed in their academic studies, military service awaited them.

"And if they send us to the border to catch spies?!" one of them conjectured.

"So what, it would be better to pretend that I hadn't seen him, let him cross! Otherwise, they'd shoot and kill me. Who needs it?" another answered, an officer's son who was also a bitchy thug.

When I was in the camp, I had heard about a Soviet secret from one of the prisoners who was a former military man: why, during thirty years after the war, hadn't Russia sent its army to participate in local wars, like the Korean War, the Vietnam War, or the war in Angola? They sent Chinese, Vietnamese, Cubans, but the Russians served at best as consultants, pilots, and operators of missile equipment.

The reason for this was that Russian propaganda exploited the joint victory in World War II to construct a myth of Russian invincibility. The secret doctrine forbade creating situations that might explode this myth, the purpose of which was to terrorize the West. For the first time, the prohibition was lifted in Afghanistan. That business ended in defeat like all the wars Russia had waged without allies: in the Crimea (1853–1856), in Japan (1904), in Poland (1920), and even in Finland (1940).

The Guards Spoke Russian

On the prisoners' train, I met Mikhailo Diyak. Among other things, his group had disseminated Lenin's promises for the independence of the nationalities and his demand to crush that independence at the right time. In Lenin's writings, it was always possible to find something, and its opposite. Unchanging, it always was and remained one thing: the thirst for rule and unlimited power by any means and at any price. All the rest were means to the end. It wasn't important which side it came from. To fulfill this historic goal—establishing absolute government in the name of rule—there needed to be a special genius for intrigue, and Lenin had that kind of genius. His life story, like the story of his party, was filled with endless intrigues, sprinkled with bloody crimes, nothing more than that.

For the first time, intrigue had been raised to the level of a science. Lenin's plan to establish the Soviet Union—brilliantly devious, a satanic trap; his "white" opponents had been incapable of understanding it. It was precisely the tsar's murderer himself who bound the nationalities with chains so that they, who had striven to rip off Russia's colonial handcuffs, would not separate. Lenin became the savior of the empire.

In Diyak's sentencing there appeared another "crime": he had tried to smash Lenin's statue with a hammer. The statue was too hard. He succeeded only in smashing the nose with much effort. The hand would by no means break. The sentence read: "...and he struck its head twice," referring to the stone statue, as if discussing a living being. We had hoped that we would be placed together in a cell in Perm, but, all of a sudden, I was placed in a solitary cell.

Diyak, a simple lad, was a man of ideals, devoid of any misgivings. He sacrificed himself, his life, in a simple routine manner, without lofty phrases, as appropriate for a man who was prepared to give himself. How many unsophisticated and unknown heroes like him have gone down to the grave! He died from cancer, which was diagnosed while he was in the camp, but they refused to cure him without "cooperation" on his part.

My new cell in the Perm prison was joined to a fantastic bathroom apparatus. This was a sort of bowl with a pipe and faucet, which was to serve both for washing and elimination. It was a hole of about five centimeters in an iron base nearly joined to the wall and the metal pipe connected to it. Only if you pressed against the cold pipe with all your strength could you situate yourself somehow by twisting your body on this impressive technological "achievement" of the Soviet Union.

The radio squawked nearly all day. However, the worst thing of all was that my cell was essentially a cockroach kingdom in every sense of the word. During a week, I slew cockroaches running on the floor, on the plank-bed, on the walls, and on the table—big ones, little ones, medium-sized ones, and teeny ones, although it seemed that they only increased and multiplied. It was as if I was battling Hydra. It seemed to me that only cockroaches remained in the world. When they left their hiding places at night, their daring increased. They scattered throughout the cell and held wedding celebrations. They dragged about and ate the corpses of their brethren. Their love games became my nightmares. Once, I swatted at one of their hiding places with a broom under the thick heating pipe, and I swept up a dead cockroach that was as white as snow from head to the tip of its tail. Aside from its color, this was a perfectly regular cockroach. I had never imagined that there were albinos among them! Several of them had developed a sixth sense. When I randomly looked at them with fatigue, they crawled about calmly and occupied themselves with their matters. However, if I had a sudden flash of thought to kill one of them, it would begin to suddenly run about agitatedly and escape beyond the heating pipe into the wall cracks before I had made any kind of movement ... for a whole week I had the privilege of enjoying this aristocratic society.

I was now taken to Kirov (the former Vyatka) and from there straight to Vladimir. Again I was in a Stolypin car. Thank goodness that they continued to hold me separately from the criminal prisoners who were sitting in the adjoining cells. When taken to the bathroom, the men and women saw each other through the bars. The women generally looked awful: drunk, ragged, tortured and corrupt. There were also others, they were a minority. The criminals, while passing the women's cage shouted: "Show a séance!"

The meaning of this was "Get undressed, show your hidden charms." The women prisoners, who were flattered, rushed to respond to the request. On both sides, bestial howls of desire were heard. It was the howl of male and female zoo animals in heat when placed in two separate, but adjacent cages. When I was taken out, the women howled: "Oh, what a young one, so juicy! Come on, look at us! My little gypsy!"

Prisoners who had been sentenced to death also traveled in the same car, bound in shackles. In the camp, they had slaughtered one of the active informers. The women pitied those brave men sentenced to death: "They're so young!"

Here I was in Kirov. Endless sitting in the squeezed, stifling small box, a half-step in length and width. Everything was contaminated, dirty; the doors, walls, and even the ceiling covered with writing. An entire world. Farewells, announcements, love requests, sayings, nicknames, greetings.

I sat there for hours until finally I was taken out to the bath house, and from there to the cell. What a cell! It was certainly a cell for those condemned to death. It was reminiscent of solitary. The small window was blocked by several rows of bars and mesh. It was impossible to reach it. It was entirely closed, covered by spider webs and dust. The cell was suffocating and didn't allow for breathing. Flies buzzed in the air. It looked like a cellar with a low and curved ceiling, which my head only hit when I stood in the middle of the narrow cell. It was almost impossible to walk about. A stone bed covered by wood on top. Thanks for nothing! Next to the door was the slop bucket, missing a handle, unbearably reeking and full of excrement. It was covered on top by a piece of cardboard. There was no faucet and no sink. The somber light of a bulb encased by iron mesh. There wasn't a drop of water, not even to wash hands with. I pounded on the door. No answer. I pounded harder, for a long time, until my fists ached.

"Fuck you! Why are you pounding my head?!" on the other side of the door the guard's lazy swearing could be heard.

"Call the commander! I deserve a normal cell!"

"Stop pounding!" the guard rebuked me, moved away, and didn't come back.

I declared a hunger strike. No response. They refused to even give me paper to write a complaint or to write my declaration of a hunger strike. They also refused to put my possessions in the cell. You're on a hunger strike—go starve yourself.

The next day, at morning inspection, the commander of the section and a doctor appeared. I informed them of my hunger strike.

"Why is this cell bad?" the woman in the white jacket shrugged her shoulders. They left. The hunger strike went on in vain. To my joy, the next day I was taken out to continue my journey.

I was again in the Stolypin. Another night on the train. For some reason, they seated me in a cell of juvenile prisoners. They told me their stories. The Soviet empire was full of prison camps for juveniles. One of them had a 13-year-old sister. She was also imprisoned for prostitution. One of them who wanted to save himself from the hands of the "legals" (camp activists), never left the punishment cells; another smashed his head on the wall with all his force so that they would move him in with the psychiatric prisoners. That's how he wanted to be saved from abuse, severe beatings and group rape.

The "crow" brought me to Vladimir Central Prison. I passed the night jailed together with the worst criminals. We were left lying on planks in the cold, exposed, next to a window shielded by a "bridle" (an obstructing metal shutter), with no pane.

Two months in solitary

The next day before noon, I was taken from the transit cell and brought before the local commanders. The usual questions, full of malicious intent and ridicule, the comments, the "recommendations," an announcement of two months of harsh imprisonment.

"Sign!"
I signed.
"What's that?!"
"A signature."

The Guards Spoke Russian

"What do you mean? What are these hieroglyphics?"

"It's Hebrew."

"He's already started!!!" yelled the officer and his paralyzed cheek, injured from shell shock, shook with anger and hatred.

I was immediately removed from the room. In the adjoining room they began a detailed search of all my possessions, my clothes, and my person. This was called "processing" in their slang. They forced me to completely strip and they searched around everything, rummaging, looking for something.

A tiny woman guard, dark-skinned and self-righteous, while writing something gave me a sidelong glance. All the women guards were shameless, like animals.

Ultimately, I too, tried to see them as domesticated animals, with no need to pay attention to them or to be embarrassed in their presence.

Once in the corridor of the prison basement, a young woman guard was sitting, red-cheeked next to the bathhouse guards. I peeked out from the dressing room and asked her to turn her face away for at least a minute, until I passed by to the wash room. Instead of answering, she placed her right palm on her left elbow and moved her arm upwards in a well-known gesture: See!

"Are you crazy?" the guards wondered. "She's here to see who's got the biggest one! All the prisoners are satisfied! What's the matter with you? Are you religious?"

After "processing," they took away all the foodstuff collected by my friends in the camp for me and led me to the cell where I was on a reduced food ration.

I was led through the wards of the enormous prison. Vladimir Central Prison appeared to me like a guard city with thousands of "residents," administrative sections, and industry. A state within a state, a kingdom of cement and iron, blocked and protected by a huge stone fence, barbed wire, watch towers, and alarm system. A true fortress of tyranny.

I found myself in a quiet solitary confinement cell. Instead of a sink and a toilet there was a smelly bucket. The cell was in one of the giant wards full of "resident" prisoners. The second ward was considered the sick ward and for some reason, it was equipped with slop buckets. Every cell looked like a bathroom.

There was a huge difference between prison and the camp. They had two different faces. I felt severance from nature the third time relatively less sharply than I had the first time. Hunger stood out more. That was the official line of punishment here. The starvation ration could not be complemented by any other source: there was no grass, no wild mushrooms, not even grasshoppers. A few tiny, salty fish, which possessed a strange odor, a ladle of a thin batter without a drop of oil, a handful of sauerkraut that caused heartburn, and 400 grams of clay-like bread—that was the daily ration I received.

There was also a psychological difference. In the camp, I had constantly felt like hunted prey, without a moment's rest. And here—there was peace. The guards were hardly ever seen. Once, I tried to stop a guard during inspection, to ask him the prison address for sending letters. No chance! I barely saw him! He peeked and disappeared like a meteor.

The number of prisoners and cells here was immeasurably greater than the number of guards, so that you would need to do something extraordinary in order to attract any attention. Furthermore, the guards were in the corridor, beyond the row of locked doors and there was no contact. In the camp, I had constantly been on the move, searching for a place where I could hide from the guards, even for a minute.

I tried to call the librarian. She approached, willingly discussing abstract subjects, promised to bring books, but she didn't bring me anything for weeks. I could only think, dream, hope and remember. Life stories from the past rose in my memory, of conflicts, nationalist confrontations, severe racism in the Soviet army, the bloody blows between Russians and Uzbecks. That had happened wherever there was a high percentage of "coloreds." Afterward, my thoughts deepened and turned inward, focused in the absolute quiet in which it was possible to hear a roach moving from its place. Suddenly—a calamity as intense as thunder. It was a guard who split the silence by passing in the corridor, striking the iron door with his big key.

The Guards Spoke Russian

At times, this sudden noise was a warning before being taken out for a walk or to the bathroom. Sometimes it was nothing more than an amusement to relieve the boredom. The prisoner flinched at the surprise and afterward, barely calmed himself as the guard continued to march back and forth thunderously.

In prison, I requested that they give me all the newspapers and magazines I had subscribed to with my money while I was still in the camp. After all, I had to read something in this endless solitude. However, Major Kotov dragged the matter out. He didn't even want to pamper me with the Soviet newspapers.

I wrote out two complaints: one to the general prosecutor's office and the other to the Ministry of Communications. Several days later, the contused captain came to me, opened the food slot, threw the envelope with the complaint at me and said:

"We have sent that one to the general prosecutor, but as for this one—nowhere! Is it clear!"

"Why? I have the right to complain there too!"

"One complaint is enough."

"It's for me to decide. Take it, please, and send it. If not, I'll have to complain about you, too."

His twisted cheek began to twitch.

"Don't forget where you are!!!" the major roared, red with anger, and slammed the window with such force that the plaster fell down from the ceiling. I hadn't heard a roar like that for a long time. It was the roar of a self-assured predatory beast.

A short time afterward, that very night, I woke up all of a sudden. Something burned and pressed on my chest. Not completely awake, I didn't understand what was happening. I was in a state of heavy, tortuous, exhausted sleep. However, sleepiness faded as the intense pain encompassed my entire being. My breathing became stifled. It was as if they had placed a fiery brick inside my chest. My pulse was almost negligible. By the dim light of the night bulb, I saw that my veins, which generally protruded, had disappeared somewhere. My palms were white as lime. I couldn't breathe. I gulped air into my mouth like a fish. I barely made it to the door and I banged with whatever strength was left. The guard answered that the doctor was not around and would only be there in the morning. When finally the medic arrived, I barely managed to get a nitroglycerine pill out of him. By chance, I remembered that the pill had helped Yagman with his heart attack, and clearly, my blood vessels were constricted. The pill saved me. I stood for some time longer against the cold wall. I placed a towel wet with water from the kettle that had cooled down over my heart. This feeling, similar to a prolonged dying, began to gradually fade away. After a short while, I was summoned to the doctor, Larisa Sukhareva, Botova's deputy.

"Nothing special," she answered when I tried to find out what it was.

Usually, solitary confinement alleviated "medical experiments." One way or another, no event connected to my heart had occurred, neither before or after. This was the one and only event that happened during the time I sat in solitary confinement for two months.

What was the value of one person's life for the empire which crushed and slew entire peoples? Because it placed itself above everything human, the natural conclusion derived from its wish to swallow up the whole earth and all within it, the ideologies, economies, social structures, and the bodies and souls of human beings.

The usual way

Feeling a vague worry, I waited for the end of the period of solitary confinement. First of all, it wasn't clear if they would leave me there, or if they would transfer me to a common cell. Secondly, only infrequently in these alleyways of the world of darkness did the unknown ever bode something pleasant. Those were my thoughts as I paced the corridors behind the guard, wondering. He moved me to the open area between buildings, to ward number one, the coldest and harshest of all with regard to discipline and nourishment. The lion's share of my imprisonment in Vladimir was spent in this ward. The summer's sun and sky were left behind me.

The Guards Spoke Russian

The prison cell.

The usual way

Through the dark corridors and chilly stairwells, I was brought to one of the innumerable cells. At the sound of the creaking door, faces looked up from the planks—terrible faces of the dead: yellow with blue-black lines under sunken eyes. Criminal prisoners? No, they were "ours," political prisoners.

One of them, whose name was Armenian but whose family had mixed and assimilated with the Russians, was in prison for an open letter of complaint to the BBC. It was about his housing problems. The second was a Ukrainian deserter from the Red Army, an agitated youth who had served on the Iranian border. The third was an adult Russian, thin and bony, slightly stooped, his arms braids of veins and sinews, his face narrow and long; his eyes darted like a wolf's from the depths of their sockets. He had a deep, ugly scar on his forehead. In its center his brain pulsed to the rhythm of his heartbeat under the thin skin.

The "dead" fell on me like vampires, lustily, to suck the fresh blood of news. They had been cut off from the world for a long time—as if in the grave. A mute terror blew from this world of graves. Its essence was expressed in the prison song sung to the Russian folk melody. Its content was "everything here is held in common—language, homeland, prison, we ourselves and even the underwear on our bodies!"

The underwear was indeed held in common then. In the bathhouse, we gave the laundry all the clothes we removed. In their place we received something washed from the general pile.

After I had told all the camp news and also of my transfer to the Urals, including everything I knew about the world beyond the barbed wire, it became my new neighbors' turn. First off, they told me about themselves and afterward about their cases. On this matter, the scarred wolf generally preferred to be silent and vague. In spite of this, he described how two escaped prisoners had wandered the roads of Siberia when suddenly, within the Siberian woods, they encountered a barbed wire fence. There were no guard towers, no dogs, no people, only a barbed wire fence surrounding two green hills in the middle of the desolate and infinite taiga. The escapees wanted to get away from this rusty fence which they thought set the boundary of an abandoned camp, when all of a sudden, they heard a strange, metallic sound. They hid again in the dense greenery. It was as if there was an opening in one of the hills, from which pairs of prisoners and their escorts began to emerge. Accompanied by the clang of shackles, they marched to the second hill and disappeared inside it. An armed guard accompanied them. The most horrible part was that not one of them made a sound. Only the clanking of iron.

In Soviet magazines, we read the words of the American communists who wrote that the Soviet Union had the "right to its daring social experiment." We were amazed at the coarse intransigence of these people. If this experiment had been tried not on someone else, but on themselves, they would be singing a different tune. However, another person's troubles don't hurt. It's wonderful and nice to sit in a comfortable apartment and philosophize about important and necessary experiments which are taking place in the lives of anonymous people at great distances, second-class people who can be victimized for the anticipated "bright future."

If that was so, how was the Nazi Mengele a criminal? Only because he belonged to the wrong party? And who was he, and by what criteria did he categorize people into types: who was the experimenter and who the guinea pig!? Indeed, it was much worse than racism. This was "the most humanistic doctrine," which reduced living people to victims of theoretical casuistry. As for the Jewish socialists, with their kibbutzim at least they had tested a social experiment only upon themselves, as befitting any true researcher. The Western communists, on the other hand, would not by any means enter their bloody "socialist camp." For some reason, it was more comfortable and quieter to look peacefully at the progress of the "experiment" from the sidelines. Or to try it at home on other citizens and never on themselves.

We also spoke about a special breed in the world of ragamuffins (with no connection to the profession itself or income level). This was a psychological category. The ragamuffins had no need of a nation, religion, family, possessions. They were the ones who were the human foundation of communism.

Bogdan Veduta related how the Soviet soldiers pursued people fleeing into Iranian territory, coarsely and arrogantly. The Iranians were afraid of disturbing them. Imaginary stories also went around that a man in one of the cells had sold his soul to the devil.

The second young one, Avakov, tried to escape life's gloom in the cell by playing chess. True, there were things to escape from. The wolf initially was alertly interested in innovations around him. He leafed through the book about the Qumran scrolls I had purchased and received in a package. Suddenly, he asked with suspicion: "Why was this book published?"

I immediately felt strange and threatened. "The authors explain the scrolls from their atheistic perspective," I replied.

"No. With the aid of this book, they suggest that Christianity is not original!" this praying wolf looked at me wrathfully.

He had the blend typical in Russia of sorrowful, criminal, and pathological asceticism. He prayed frequently and fervently. Despite being in prison, he strictly kept the fasts. He also cursed using the filthiest language possible. Sinful behavior erupted from within him, he hated everybody with an intense hatred burning deeply in his sunken eyes, in his terrible, narrow face. However, he especially hated Jews. He suspected nearly everyone of hiding their origin. For entire days, he either lay inert like a board, his eyes glowing with a dark splendor, or paced from corner to corner, building up his hatred. This mute accumulation of internal evil, we felt physically. Indeed, when he became aware of my views on the question of nationality, he truly became a predatory beast. After a series of coarse hooligan teasing, he moved on to direct terror.

When we read about the Yom Kippur War in the newspaper, I turned on the radio to hear the latest news (in this cell, the radio had a switch). Without a word, the wolf stood up and crossed over to the shelf of dishes. I immediately felt that something was wrong, but I didn't show my fears. The wolf came up close to me, still silent, and suddenly landed a forceful blow on my head with a metal bowl he held with both hands. I managed to pull the bowl out of his hands at the right moment, and it rolled onto the floor.

The situation was idiotic. On the one hand, I had to defend myself; on the other hand, I couldn't allow him to drag me into an

The Guards Spoke Russian

altercation. The guards were waiting for something like this to add more time to my term; this time for a criminal cause. Under the skin of his split forehead, his brain could be seen. If something touched that spot, he would face certain death. Afterward, they could sentence me to death for "murder." If he remained alive, that would be a problem too. I knew all of these characters. Before I had arrived at Vladimir, a Ukrainian nationalist named Semenyuk was there, who occasionally expressed nationalist sentiments, thus arousing the wrath of Bikov, his cellmate.

At night, when everyone was asleep, Bikov took a metal bowl, stole over to Semenyuk's plank, and struck his head with all his strength. Fortunately, the blow only hit him next to the temple. Semenyuk's first words when he raised himself from his bed were: "Why did you hit me?!" Incomprehension and amazement were greater than the intense pain and bitterness.

Usually in every cell there was someone close to the guards, one of "theirs." Despite the fact that twice a day during inspection, the guards saw the prisoner's battered head, no reaction occurred regarding this incident. They were obligated to respond to that immediately. But what for? They continued to hold the prisoners together in the cell, as if nothing had happened. If one of "theirs" was victorious—excellent. And if not—it wasn't so bad: it was always possible to add more prison time to the "nationalist," or even execute him. Besides, it was such a convenient situation for "re-education!" Political prisoners devouring each other like crabs in a barrel! The KGB's dream!

I didn't have much time for hesitation. My reaction would have to be immediate. I grabbed my enemy's wrists, tightened my hands over them. While avoiding his attempts to strike me with his head or legs, I began to find out what he wanted from me. It became clear that he merely wanted me to turn off the radio. I held him somewhat longer until he calmed down, and afterward, I fulfilled his modest request.

At the same moment, Avakov muttered in annoyance: "What kind of a thing is this, to attack someone with a bowl, for no reason?"

Instead of an answer, the wolf bent over, lifted the utensil under his bed, and without a superfluous word, attacked Avakov. The quarrel began. At that time, a fourth prisoner was in our cell: Slava Mirkushev, the great mystic, my acquaintance from the past and cellmate in Mordovia. He recovered first and began to separate the hawks. The guard who had been alerted by the noise, opened the food window and began to accompany the events with threats. The wolf continued his attempts to renew the battle, without paying attention to anything.

Ultimately, additional guards arrived and they invited all the cell's inhabitants to a "clarification," one by one. I didn't know what to do. The wolf in the cell and the guards outside the cell, an enemy here and an enemy there. I said that I didn't know anything and hadn't seen anything. Avakov and Mirkushev told everything, because they didn't want to stay in the same cell with someone dangerous. Avakov also didn't want to be punished for the sins of someone else. The wolf was removed from the cell. We could breathe freely. This was truly salvation.

Several days later, we were taken to the bathhouse. All of a sudden the door of the narrow washroom opened, and our acquaintance with the lupine gleam in his sunken eyes entered. Without saying a word, he took one of the dirty bowls and began to bathe. Deathly silence spread over the place. Satan's hands held a bowl of boiling hot water. Against all official orders, the guards had put him with those he had a quarrel with. Generally, they would get us out of the bathhouse as quickly as possible. This time we all washed and bathed endlessly, and afterward, we banged at length on the doors to call the guards to take us out. When I returned to the cell, I wrote a complaint to the general prosecutor that the prison administration purposely created provocative situations which could lead to murderous confrontations. I didn't mention details or names. However, the following day, the wolf was removed from the cell after having been returned to our company via the bathhouse. They asked me to rescind my complaint, because the "problem had been solved."

The cell is flooded

I would like to tell about a common occurrence in the prison cells on the ground floor in Vladimir. Angela Davis (the American

The Guards Spoke Russian

communist arrested for murder) never encountered anything like this. If she had, it would have been engraved in fiery letters on the tablets of world history. But this did happen to us. After all, we were only simple mortals, not members of the "Holy Communist Church." Therefore, justifiably so, we were under the saving protection of the new Inquisition—the KGB—the Russian Gestapo.

Consecutive days never passed in cell 16 of the first ward without hearing a noisy bubbling in the toilet. The sewage water in the toilet rose from the clogged sewage pipes somewhere under the floor of the cell. The water filled the toilet, spilling over into the cell. We used to run to the door, bang on it, and shout, demanding that they close the faucets. The guards would only begin seriously paying attention to what was happening when the filth rose over the cell's threshold and invaded the corridor. Only then did the prisoner-plumbers open the sewage pipes and clean them. When we were taken out for our daily walk, we were afraid to leave possessions on the floor lest they float away in our absence on a foul sea.

The moment the routine communist "flood" began, we took books and possessions out from under the beds (there was no other room to store them in the crowded cells), we climbed on the plank with our shoes, and sadly looked down where the putrid liquids rose and spread—with "torpedoes" of defecation inside them as well as other "pleasant" remains. Our double captivity continued for hours. When the clogged pipe had been opened, it was the obligation of the person on-duty in the cell to step down from the plank to collect the filth and place it in the toilet again with whatever means available. Afterward, he had to flood the cell with clean water several times, wash and scrub the floor, and again haul up the dirty water into the toilet until the odors dissipated a bit. However, everything quickly repeated itself.

All of us took turns and exchanged places daily. Those who were on-duty when the communist floods occurred felt particularly angry, seeing this as the hand of fate. Thus, for example—I still remember as if it were only yesterday—Slava Mirkushev's bald head, shining below in the faint light of the electric bulb, plodding about in that hell, bending over the stench, hauling liquid until his arms and back

The cell is flooded

ached while we looked on from above. Afterward, others replaced him.

Slava's fate was fraught with even more wondrous signs. Since childhood, Slava had felt that he was the focus of mystical forces. In the camp, this phenomenon reached its height. Now, while he was in prison, his "guru," Vandakurov, had been liberated from the camp. However, the situation only worsened. He was convinced that terrible things were about to happen, that Vandakurov and others like him had put themselves at the service of the Bolsheviks, that in their secret laboratory, they were preparing a secret super-weapon, and they were using Slava as their guinea pig.

Slava imagined that somewhere beneath his forehead, a "receiver" operated. There weren't always broadcasts. However, in their absence, there was a background buzz, like that of a generator. Sometimes the "receiver" was in operation, and Slava heard words in his mind. He saw complete pictures or unusual situations he couldn't describe in words. Once, at the end of a séance, he heard in his mind the typical sound "Ta ... la ... la," like the sound of a recording tape. Sometimes the sounds beckoned him to converse.

To tell the truth, I didn't believe him. I thought the guy simply was suffering from hallucinations. However, later on, when I got permission to leave the Soviet Union, I heard on the Voice of America broadcast about a secret Soviet weapon that worked by strange microwave radiation directed at the American embassy. The broadcast told of what this radiation did to people's mental functioning—the appearance of sounds and words which caused a lack of concentration and might even cause heart attacks. The Americans kept the basic information secret. It seemed that science had achieved such precision that it overlapped magic. We stood on the brink of a mystical world which would infiltrate our lives like the physical world. Super-espionage would be created: receiving information directly from the brain, without verbal or written connection. A weapon had been created capable of paralyzing the opponent even before he could use any means of physical defense.

Two to three times during the 1970s, the Russians placed the army on full alert in order to invade China. They planned to destroy the main Chinese centers with atomic weapons, to cut off Xinjiang, Manchuria, Inner Mongolia and Tibet. The aim was to send China back to the Stone Age, pushing it toward the sea with an iron ring of new satellite states. However, something always interrupted the plan, and the heightened readiness was cancelled. In the meantime, the Chinese already had the means for a crushing counterattack.

The Russians therefore chose another way: they worked on a mysterious super-weapon against which no one had means of defense. They thought that under the cover of détente, when development would be in the final stages, they would set out on world conquest. I had heard from many sources that people with mystical capabilities had frequently vanished the minute their capabilities had been made known to the authorities, and that secret research institutes were working within the Soviet Union on hypnosis and magic.

Once, in the workplace smoking room in Camp 19 in Mordovia, Slava went to make tea for himself and Vandakurov. Suddenly, Vandakurov made a strange circular movement; Slava stopped in the middle of walking, as if his right leg and left arm had been paralyzed. Vandakurov made another motion and the "paralyzed" limbs again began to move, followed by the other two limbs becoming paralyzed. With a third movement, the "teacher" restored his shocked pupil to his usual state.

"How do you do it?" cried Slava. He was prepared to suffer anything to learn the method.

"Ha, ha, ha," the bald Mephistopheles laughed in his cracked voice, and wrote some secret formula in his notebook.

There is a magical maneuver in Raja yoga (a special kind of yoga): inhaling through one nostril and exhaling through the other. Experts know how to do that automatically; every so often the procedure begins with the other nostril. During Slava's conversations with Vandakurov, he heard the characteristic sound of this change several times. The latter not only spoke, but penetrated deeply within the soul of his conversation partner. At the beginning of their acquaintance, Vandakurov lectured Slava about the doctrine of the twelve Aryan gods, led by Thor, who planned to create a world. The thirteenth god was eavesdropping upon them. He created the world in his own way in order to concentrate rule in his hands. As such, he preceded the other twelve gods. The Aryan gods were now rescuing their people from the terrible Jewish world that had been built by the rebel.

The celestial struggle between the gods was reflected in the struggle between the Aryans and the Jews in this world. This struggle would develop and intensify to a decisive, culminating confrontation. Relating this, Vandakurov made sudden up and down movements with his hand. As if waving a conductor's baton, he concentrated all Slava's life force, his strength increased and he struck his head. Vandakurov motioned downward with his hand, and immediately ceased this horrible illumination. Slava, shaken up, agitated, trembling, didn't know what to do with himself and didn't understand what had happened to him. The world of magic both frightened and tempted him. He also wanted to become a wonder worker. He thirstily tried to learn everything he could, to try it out on others, and submerged himself in a trance.

The cellmates complained about Slava's hypnotic effect, and sometimes a conflict arose. I behaved simply. The moment I felt that something was wrong, I prayed inwardly, and everything passed as though nothing had ever been.

Once I was praying with especially great tension of will, but completely in silence, without making a sound. Slava was sitting on his bed in the lotus position, with a blanket covering his head. This helped him enter a trance. All of a sudden, he threw off the blanket, turned to me and said, "What are you doing there?"

"Nothing," I answered innocently.

"That's not true. I feel the force coming from you. It ruined my trance. Do you know magic?"

"No, it's forbidden to us."

However, Slava didn't believe me. I was in shock—that was truly an extra-sensory link.

Once, at night, Slava saw a spirit in the form of a brown shadow enter the cell. He was certain that it was the soul of one of those maguses sending signals to his brain, removing his soul from his body, and sometimes accompanying it all with frightening explanations. Slava suddenly found himself in some kind of invisible square box, whose sides glowed like a red hot wire. This invisible obstacle prevented the "brown" from reaching him. Nevertheless, somehow the brown ghost managed to tear the "wire" and afterward struck Slava with something directly in his heart.

"Know this!" said the "brown" thing in fury to his victim writhing with intense pain, and disappeared.

In the last days of inhabiting the cell which occasionally flooded with filth, Slava was summoned for an interview with the prison psychiatrist, Valentin Rogov. Slava was most surprised by the fact that Rogov was totally aware of what was going on. He was only interested in a few details. A short time after we had been transferred to another cell, Slava was hospitalized. After that, in ward 12 (for the mentally ill) in Mordovia, and following that in the psychiatric hospital in Dnepropetrovsk, where Plusch also stayed, the famous Ukrainian fighter for human rights.

The move was totally unexpected. Preceding it, Avakov was released, because he had served his term of imprisonment. They ordered all the residents of the cell to organize themselves with their possessions. They first took Bogdan. Afterward, they led me and Slava together to the third ward, to a large cell. Our amazement increased upon again seeing our unforgettable wolf! The tension increased.

The cell was on the top floor. Water didn't reach it at all or only in a thin trickle. The toilet caused terrible problems. The wolf soon returned to his evil ways, threatening murder. He accused Slava and me of every sin in the world. According to him, we were the ones who had attacked him without cause! For some reason, I remembered Finland's "invasion" of the Soviet Union in 1940, as well as Israeli "aggression." I declared a hunger strike, and by no means would I respond to the enemy's provocations. The ward commander arrived, opened the food window and asked what the reason was for my hunger strike.

"I demand transfer to another cell, and an end to the provocations."

"Who's being provocative?"

"Your administration!"

The window slammed shut, and the wolf immediately retreated. For a while longer, the guards pretended that they didn't understand,.

Triangle

Afterward, they removed him. In his place, they brought Bogdan. Feeling the anti–Semitic atmosphere, he almost pretended as if he didn't know me. Well then, it wasn't the first time I had met friends like that.

They suddenly ordered me to appear with my possessions. Why? What for? I met the wolf again in the corridor; he was being led in my direction. How? Again?

Triangle

But no, they put him in the watch room and led me further. Stairs, corridors, squeaking and slamming iron doors; clear skies above as they moved me from ward to ward. Only at such moments was it possible to see the sky the way it should be seen, and not as narrow checkerboard squares. Again to the first ward, third floor. The tiny, triangular cell. It was impossible to move about; there was no room to pace. The planks, a small table, and the slop bucket took up nearly all the space. There was no plumbing and no running water. Seats were built into the wall next to the table; only a child could use them. The wall hindered sitting, and two people had to sit contortedly. There was no room for a third person. He would have to eat wherever he could, sitting on the bed.

One of my new neighbors, Igor Ogurtsov, a known leader of regime oppositionists, was the dominant personality. The other was a deserter named Trepov. It turned out that initially Bogdan had been added to the cell. Afterward, they removed him and the wolf took his place. Ogurtsov, who had been provoked by the wolf many times in the past, provocations which had ended in brawls, adamantly refused to stay in the same cell with him. Therefore, the wolf was sent back to the third ward, and they brought me here. Thank God. It was possible to breathe freely.

It was better off without a faucet and sink, and with a slop bucket, than with that monster. Ogurtsov was a veteran prisoner. He said that up until recently, wolves like that had determined the prison environment. Some of them were really in the service of the KGB. Others simply did what they did because of their evil nature. Ogurtsov, the prison KGB commander, often placed an undesirable prisoner in a cell full of such human filth. Afterward he would summon the man driven to despair, turning to him amiably:

"So, maybe you're sorry? Maybe you'll cooperate? You'll help us and we'll help you."

In the past, Ogurtsov invited all the political prisoners to see him, one by one. He made an offer to each one to become an informer. Instead of saying "hello," he immediately threw out "Do you want to eat?"

Or "Do you want a woman?"

When he called Trepov, he made a joke out of his name which means "chatterbox": "Come on, let's c-h-a-t-t-e-r a bit?"

The prisoners told each other these things, which created a stir. Ogurtsov "went into the underground" and continued to strike—not a frontal attack, but behind the scenes. He didn't grant me the favor of even an appearance. Ogurtsov explained a large part of the corruption of even the political prisoners, saying that everyone tried to establish normal relations with Moscow, as if nothing special was happening. Therefore the banditry was legitimized as it were, and was considered the norm.

Was it possible to wonder then that it had spread far and wide? Its opposite was the phenomenon to wonder at. In spite of this, how, in this scorched earth, did seeds of opposition and a disagreement sprout? Where did people draw the courage to emerge with only their bare hands against the invincible iron monster? Indeed, the weak and restrained encouragement to regime opponents came from the outside and was encouragement in word only, whereas the monster received bread, dollars, an abundance of machinery, astonishing all who saw it from those fans, the opposing "sympathizers." True tribute! It was impossible to call by any other name the billions in credit transferred to this serial, professional bankrupt. What self-humiliation before an open enemy of the free world! What encouragement!

Criminal-political

C. severed relationships with his dysfunctional family early, and amused himself with brawling and drunkenness. Once, when he returned home as drunk as Lot, he "saw" a giant cat, as big as a man, on his bed. C. ran outside as fast as he could. It's no wonder that he continued downhill until arriving at the camp for criminal prisoners, where he also carried on and saw and experienced different and unusual atrocities. For example, before his eyes prisoners threw an ostracized prisoner into a huge tank of boiling water.

After that, for the crime of waving a flag decorated with a swastika, he began to be moved around between the camps for political prisoners. With an inborn acting talent, he impersonated an educated person, a superior being, a warrior, a saint; who knows what else. He swallowed books wholesale, feverishly, but skipped over a lot.

He perceived himself as a know-it-all. He related to every accomplishment of the most minor and insignificant sort maliciously; perceiving it as an attempt on his life. He particularly enjoyed slander. In his eyes, everyone was inferior. He alone stood above everyone. It seemed to him that the entire world was focused on him. If someone looked at him—it was a sign that he was jealous. If no one looked at him—hatred. If someone gazed downward—he was plotting something. And if he directed his gaze upward—he was being arrogant! Every breath, sound, movement, or word of his fellow man was received as a wicked plot. There were even hallucinations, songs from the past induced by an alcoholic fever. He avenged himself on those around him, if he thought they were denigrating him. The guards skillfully exploited his condition: blackmailing him with threats that he would never be released, while, at the same time, as an opening for salvation, embedding within him clear suggestions.

One day, shaking his head at me, he let slip that he felt the need to murder someone, and then "they'll release me, or something else…." And once I must say he was on the verge of executing his plot. There was no knowing what stopped him. All ideologies in the world were mixed up in the chaos of his destructive, evil, and vile heart. Once this Cain, who thought of himself as a Christian, revealed a secret idea which he had been nurturing: "People have lost a lot by abstaining from cannibalism!"

The second cellmate thought barbarically that there was no reason to restrain himself, and held everything cheap, even his fate. At least he had a wild nobility. He wouldn't attack anyone from behind or in his sleep—but C. was capable of that. He once planned to spill a container of boiling water on his neighbor and to scald him from head to foot. It's possible to wonder about the inquisitorial sophistication demonstrated by the KGB when they chose my cellmates. In the past, I had spent almost a year with prisoners who were all criminals, but never had I suffered so bitterly.

A Chinese meal

In 1974, exotic hieroglyphics were discovered in the prison yards.

When taken for a walk or to another cell, we sometimes encountered groups of Chinese who were being led somewhere. Ultimately, a Chinese prisoner encountered us in our cell. This was Yu Xi Lin, a refugee falsely accused of spying for China in order to force him to spy (in reality) for Russia. Initially, he feared laying out the details of his accusation. Instead of this, we discussed how to save ourselves from starvation, especially from our lack of protein. Occasionally, they provided us with small salty marsh fish, which were rusty, rotten and putrid, and caused food poisoning. There was no other protein. When such "food" is thrown at prisoners for months, the hunger for protein becomes insufferable. Bodily functions such as temperature regulation are disrupted; a person burns up with fever or trembles with cold; the feeling of hunger becomes the only sensation, existing in every cell in the body. Soon, the prisoner begins to suffer irreversible pathological changes.

In his garbled Russian, Yu Xi Lin wrote a complaint that not even a pig would eat these fish. (He called the hefty prison doctor Butova "Pork.") At first, there was no reaction. However, when the protest became a mass one, the authorities responded with solitary confinement. Gunar Rodeh, myself and many others were thrown into solitary for seven days.

We were saved by the fact that there was nothing blocking our cell's window. Up until recently, the cell had been used as the guards' office. Beyond the window bars there was clear sky! This miracle could not be missed. The Chinese prisoner and I began by weaving thin ropes and making loops out of thread. We scattered bread crumbs on the window and quickly caught a fat pigeon in our trap. We put it in a sack and immediately hid it under the bed. We conferred about how to secretly cook it. Just then, a letter arrived with a message about Silva Zalmanson's release! I was so happy that we granted amnesty to the pigeon and liberated it.

But we didn't restrain ourselves with the next one. We ate it. We cooked it in pieces in an aluminum cup set to boil by burning newspaper. There was a risk that a guard would catch us and we would again be punished with solitary. We organized the perfect camouflage. The mattress hid the "kitchen" in the corner farthest from the door, at the end of the bed, under which we set afire consecutive delicate rolls of newspaper under the cup. One of us guarded the door, listening for the guard's footsteps. These pieces of meat filled our bodies with renewed strength. Before we were moved to another cell, we managed to eat two more pigeons that had been nesting on the prison roof.

News of the imprisonment

Guards behind the barbed-wire fences plundered the prisoners' "free" (mainly their civilian clothing) possessions' storeroom, and afterward, staged a fire in there. We wouldn't receive any compensation—the court wasn't even so kind as to consider our demand. When we had been leaving Mordovia, a forest of television antennas rose above the guards' houses. They became rich at our expense. The storeroom looting signaled that it was now their colleagues' turn in the Urals.

The human composition of my new cellmates changed from its previous composition—half criminal—to its new composition—mostly political. This transition came about as a result of organized opposition in the camps against the hangmen.

The big strike in Camp 36, in reaction to the guards' beating of Stepan Sapeliyak, a young Ukrainian prisoner, and mass strikes and hunger strikes in Camp 35, symbolized a sharp turning point in the atmosphere, a change which had been in process for a while and finally erupted.

One of the forms of protest in the camps was suicide. In Camp 35, an old Ukrainian, Opanasenko, had committed suicide, leaving a note behind: "Hangmen, be damned!" Joseph Meshner, a Jew, was taken out of the loop and barely saved. However, our situation was immeasurably better than it had been. Once, they had kept all the prisoners together—men and women, and there even had been a joint bathroom. Women prisoners had been so starved that the skin of their concave stomachs sagged like a surplus apron over their thighs. There were only about seventy prisoners who were well-connected. They used to hire women prisoners for a piece of bread and the miserable women would hastily swallow the bread in the midst of having sex. Now the guards had begun to aspire to a resurrection of the atrocities.

Not far from us there was the "blacksmiths" cell. They essentially worked as professional torturers for an extra ladle of porridge. Occasionally, heartrending screams emerged from there. The guards only chuckled. Officially, a prisoner who didn't toe the line was transferred to that cell. In fact, he was thrown into the brutal hands of the "porridge mercenaries," who would punish him harshly, damage his kidneys, break his bones, and rape him.

Afterward, the victim would be taken out and replaced by the next in line. Many times we couldn't sleep at night: someone in the neighboring cell was knocking repeatedly on the door, begging to be taken out of the cell in which he was about to be abused. The guards made a laughingstock out of this and sometimes they even moved the "bothersome" prisoner from his cell and delivered murderous blows to him in the corridor or in solitary. Major Kiselyov excelled at this. He beat several prisoners to death. That's how the prisoner Gerasimov, nicknamed "wild man," was killed. His corpse was dragged from solitary. They recorded that he died a "natural" death. The muffled, bloodcurdling blows reached our ears, and the inhuman death cries, until everything became silent.

Once, in 1975, in ward 3 of Vladimir Prison, a Jewish criminal prisoner, Boris Guliyaka from Leningrad, jumped out of the hostile cell where they sought his murder, and refused to go back. He requested to be transferred to another cell. Instead of that, a mass rabble of guards gathered around him and began to shove him back into his cell forcibly. He demonstrated passive resistance. When they had already managed to push him past the door, the guard, a mustachioed thug, kicked him in the groin with all his might.

Guliyaka lost consciousness. Initially, he wasn't able to move or to urinate. Despite his pleas, a doctor wasn't sent to see him. Even the hostile criminal prisoners, who were human beasts, showed themselves to be more humane: they laid their victim down on a bed and didn't harm him again.

"I'd like to die"

During a precious pause after rough incidents and a prolonged hunger strike, accompanied by the tortures of violent forced feeding, quiet prevailed in the cell. From the bed of Volodiya Afanasyev rose the occasional half-histrionic, half melancholy cry: "I'd like to die!"

Volodiya was small, gaunt, and good-natured. He possessed a sense of humor and was an advocate of the truth. He was a simple lad from the Russian poor, who had been drafted into the army and had served in the building corps. An atmosphere of drunkenness and lust prevailed in the corps. Prostitutes filled the barracks. Each unit in rotation spent time with the prostitute, sometimes right on the table. The woman only fondled the head of the "lover" on duty. When she discovered a freshly-shaved head of a recruit, she would drive him out with a shove: "Greenhorn! Next!"

A lack of discipline, excess drinking and leaving the base without permission were routine. The commanders had to somehow frighten the rowdy soldiers, to put a stop to the unruly behavior. That's how Volodiya Afanasyev and his friend fell into their hands.

Both of them were from the Urals, and were also serving in the Urals, which was a rarity. Occasionally, they would take off and go home, to the village of their birth, to their mothers.

On one of these disappearances, they were caught drunk on a train. To deter the others, they were accused of being traitors to the homeland and escaping abroad! That's how the commanders intended to impose order, to sacrifice those two lives for "an educational act." Whoever has a bit of geographical knowledge knows that nowhere in the continent-spanning empire is there a more remote place from the borders than the Urals. It was there that they had evacuated the factories during the war. To escape from there was perhaps possible only by way of the North Pole...

However, trifles such as geography didn't bother the regime. Volodiya got his ten years and became "political." Although he hadn't misbehaved in the camp, because of his participation in the opposition he was sent to Vladimir Prison.

Already during transfer, he had encountered Yatsishin, who he had known in Camp 35. Yatsishin had also behaved in a strange manner in the camp. He distanced himself from everyone, and claimed that a microphone had been embedded in his hat. He saw enemies and agents in those who tried to reassure him. However, there were also more severe incidents. Once, he maintained that the Mordovian woods around the camp were not forests but cardboard scenery, and that the camp was essentially situated in the middle of Moscow and he was its only prisoner. All the rest were undercover KGB agents following him.

Instead of curing him, they sent Yatsishin to solitary confinement again and again, which only made his condition more severe.

"I'd like to die"

On journeys, Yatsishin asked Volodya if the KGB could place a telescope inside a lamp.

Volodiya tried with all his might to calm Yatsishin. However, at Vladimir the distance between buildings, and the hallways supervised by closed-circuit monitors, were manifest. Yatsishin looked at his neighbor here and "understood" what was happening. In addition to Volodiya and Yatsishin, Simas Kudirka, David Chernoglaz, and Vladimir Bukovsky sat in the cell with them. Yatsishin began to hallucinate, and then folded himself up into a fetal position.

"He'll eat shit soon enough!" prophesized Bukovsky, who the Bolsheviks had turned into an expert in psychiatry after imprisoning him in psychiatric hospitals for regime opponents. In fact, immediately afterward, that horror began. His companions struggled with him as much as they could, but his maniacal strength was enormous. He used to stand straight as a pole and then fall flat on the floor. The sound of his full height striking the concrete floor was terrible. Giant, blue bruises swelled on his forehead. His companions had to make a super-human effort to force the psychiatrist to give Yatsishin attention, to recognize his disease and transfer him to the prison's hospital. The psychiatrist was too busy with the sane. Later on, as a result of a reorganization of prisoners in the different cells, Volodiya ended up sitting in a cell with another disturbed individual; Lazariev was his name. He was only crazy on the subject of anti–Semitism. As far as he was concerned, everyone around him was a Jew, from prisoners to guards.

"I know your secret!" he shouted to his two Russian cellmates. Once they were taken for their daily walk and Lazariev remained in the cell. One of the guards wanted to enter the cell for some reason and opened the door. Thinking that his cellmates had returned, Lazariev attacked the person entering the cell with the toilet lid, raised to deliver the blow while wildly howling: "I'll k-k-k-ill the damned Jews!" The guard almost had a stroke and barely managed to slam the cell door shut.

After the hunger strike, Abankin was again moved to our cell. He was a fervent sportsman, and even in prison he tried to exercise. Once, he did a handstand on the table and suddenly tumbled off with wild laughter, endangering his life. It turned out that while standing on his hands, he had read something written in pencil on the newspaper spread out on the table as a substitute tablecloth: "I am spirit, I am a man"; "All men are spirits."

That was how Volodiya practiced logic after devouring Kant. "I am spirit" became the motto of the cell.

"Would you like to die?" we asked more than once. "And is a forest a plant?" Volodiya asked, after Kant's writings had totally addled his brain.

During this period, they began to "industrialize" the prison and forced us to work.

The temperature in the work cell was 10 degrees centigrade. In spite of the electrical equipment, the cell was damp. The concrete floor was on a slant, so we sat in a contorted position. Our machines were supposed to rumble until the small hours of the night, even when the prison had gone to sleep. However, the nature of the work particularly aroused our suspicion. Incarceration is any way a risk factor for vision. There is always half-darkness. Eyes aren't used in prison for seeing distances. On all sides, there are only nearby walls, a window blocked by iron, barred, tight netting over the small exercise yard. All day there was minimal artificial, yellow lighting by a 60-watt incandescent lamp. After all of this, they forced us to weld together tiny electronic components, and even the work cell had a barred window and an incandescent lamp. They absolutely refused to put fluorescent lights in our cell, as had been placed in the work cells of the criminal prisoners. No reason was given for the refusal. The aim was clear: to damage our vision. Along with this, our food completely lacked vitamins and we were forbidden to have them sent from outside. Our allotment of fish oil had been stopped. If you don't want to see the world in the official light, so, become blind and you won't see a thing!

Nearly the entire first floor of the first ward now consisted of criminal prisoners. Despite the prohibition by Soviet law, their cells were organized for habitation as well as for work.

In a cell filled to the brim, a simple Soviet criminal sat on his plank. There was a machine in front of him, and he put out product day and night (zippers, electronic components). To his right—a toilet. To his left—a plate of mush. What else does a man need in order to be perfectly happy? Wasn't this paradise on earth? The epitome of the worker's paradise!

When we renounced this happiness, we were punished in solitary and ultimately transferred to the third ward, to the nutrition cell. There, each one of us received 400 grams of damp, clay-like bread per day. During the starvation days of the war, German captives had been given 600 grams of bread. However, we were guilty of ideological "crimes" that were immeasurably more serious!

Next to our new location, a rebellion took place in the criminal cell. From above, with an improvised rope, a small package of Mahorka (home-made tobacco) was lowered to them. The prisoner Vasyukov, standing opposite the window, freed the gift sent by his friend in the cell above. At that very moment, the red-faced guard Sukharyov, who resembled a gorilla, burst into the cell. He saw what was going on. Before anyone could blink an eye, Sukharyov was next to the window. He fell upon the "wrongdoer" and began to strangle him with his enormous arms. The prisoners barely managed to save their faint friend from this vise-like grip. Furiously, they shoved Sukharyov out of the cell. It had seemed that the incident was over. But it was not! The door opened and a drunken officer beat the first prisoner he encountered. The cell was large and densely populated; they kicked the officer out too.

All of a sudden, the tapping of many feet was heard. The prisoners discovered through the slit in the door that a mass of guard cadets were approaching their cell. It was clear that now they would be punished. All the prisoners would be beaten until disabled or until dead. The prisoners barricaded the door, breaking up beds and window frames into sticks and rods for self-defense. Similarly, they broke the windowpanes out of fear that the guards would use gas. On their journeys, our guys had often met criminal prisoners, half-crazed from nerve gas used against them. In this event, they took wet towels to breathe through. The prisoners in the cell declared that they would defend themselves to the end. The siege went on until the small hours of the night. After midnight, the prison commander, Zavyalkin, arrived with the Vladimir city prosecutor.

They promised not to use force or implement any judinial reprisal of the prisoners if they lay down "their arms." They agreed. They were transferred from the destroyed cell to another one, and afterward, they were dispersed and quickly judged. All the prisoners were given additional sentences, but no one of the violent guards was brought to trial. I remember the names of two of those sentenced: Vladimirov and Vasiyokov. The rebellion was in May 1975.

Working flesh

The surveys say that in 1948 there were 18 million prisoners in the Soviet Union. The turnover among prisoners was rather high, particularly because of the high death rate from hunger, cold, disease, and sanitary-medical neglect. The Soviet prisoner had every reason to envy animals. The reason for this situation was the value scale. The government, its maintenance, expansion, and entrenchment were of the highest value there. During the communist era it was raised to the level of idolatry with theft and murder at its foundation. The place of a man on this scale was at the bottom, together with nature. Man and nature were a kind of free resource (to differentiate from animals, which had a price). Therefore, the destructive, exhausting and draining exploitation, lacking basic conditions (which also had a price, and that would be an unnecessary waste), had become the foundation of the slave economy.

The prisoners would do hard labor, but there was no need to build for them orderly homes and services, or to provide them with appropriate clothing and food. They could settle for waste that belonged in the garbage can. They were available and mobile: the scope of arrests would be conducted according to a five-year plan, according to needs, and the "working flesh" would flow without problem anywhere required, even to the North Pole. The working flesh would enclose itself within barbed wire, would build huts, and work like a mule for a plate of miserable mush. There was no need to ensure safety: limitless new ones would come to replace the killed or wounded. There was no need for sophisticated food: mush was cheaper. Whoever compared the state of these prisoners to slaves was bitterly mistaken; a slave was bought for money. Therefore, there was an incentive to protect his relative health and welfare, like a beast or an object is protected. The prisoner was free of cost, and he always had a replacement. All the vast building of communism was executed over the bones of the prisoners. They were the spearhead of the Soviet economy. Iron rails beyond the Arctic Circle, gold mines in Kolyma, coal in Vorkuta, copper in Karaganda, oil and gas pipelines, the huge dams—the glory of the regime—had been purchased with the torture and death of prisoners.

More than once, amputated human fingers or hands were found among the logs from Siberia sold to England. This was a mute and terrifying reminder of the source of this wood. They didn't even "waste" those condemned to death, but exploited them for a while in uranium mines until they died from radiation.

And the miserable and submissive slaves in the big camp, which was the Soviet empire, surrounded by barbed wire, were prepared to sell their souls in order to save themselves from the fate of the prisoners. Anyone who tried to escape from "this earthly paradise" was accused of treason and his doom was sealed: a maximum prison term or even execution—that was the sentence of the escaped slave.

The monastery of silence

Vasil Fedorenko was last arrested in Czechoslovakia.

He was on his way to Germany where his sister lived, after the authorities hadn't responded to his requests for permission to travel to see her. Previously, he had been imprisoned in the Chmelnitsky monastery which had become a prison. He was given special work to do there, worse than our work, even though it didn't lead to smashed fingers or lungs filled with cancerous chemical dust like at our place. This prison-monastery had first been heard of during the guerrilla period in western Ukraine. Peasants from the neighboring villages had been sent there together with their families. No one had returned from there. Words chiseled into the walls had been preserved, such as: "Hey, hello, Katarina! Watch over the children!" Horrible screams pierced the walls of the monastery. Fedorenko and a bunch of prisoners had been sent there many years later. Their job was to pull bodies out of the basements which had been flooded and sealed. There was no end of male, female and children's skeletons whose skulls had been smashed.

In Vladimir, Vasil was sent to solitary in critical condition at the time of the prolonged hunger strike. This had been done according to orders by the Interior Ministry which allowed sending prisoners from the hospital to solitary without any regard for the severity of their condition.

The medicine in the prison hospital either didn't exist or was past the expiration date. There was an absolute prohibition on packages of medicine or vitamins being sent by relatives, even if without them, the prisoner would certainly die. Even after difficult operations, the prisoners would be thrown into locked cells without any services or assistance. If the post-surgery prisoner was lucky, he might have a cellmate who could and would help. Even a dying person was not allowed to receive food from relatives—not even the most basic food.

When a corpse was removed from a place of imprisonment, the dead man's heart had to be pierced and the skull had to be shattered with an iron bar. In that manner, the authorities prevented possible impersonation in order to evade imprisonment. The corpse wasn't given to the family. The place of burial was a state secret.

Jacob and the cannibal

When I had ended my "career" in the prison factory and was sent to solitary, the drought of May 1975 was at its height. Fires broke out everywhere. Again the Bolsheviks put their hopes in manna from

America, which had never disappointed them. In solitary, it's routine to suffer from the cold, but now that such a stifling heat wave prevailed, it was preferable to lie down naked on the concrete floor.

The solitary cell was closed and sealed: a double window on one side and a double door opposite it. I would have broken the panes, but I couldn't do it because of the bars obstructing me.

The only possible occupation was to converse with the prisoner in the adjacent solitary cell. He was one of the "striped" political prisoners (the habitual offenders stood out in their striped uniforms, which were copied from those of the prisoners in the Nazi concentration camps. I was never entirely sure that the East was the one that had copied the West and not the reverse).

This neighbor related that most of the prisoners in their group were indeed the most hopeless. Not finding their place among the criminal repeaters like themselves, ostracized as the criminal of the criminals, they were forced to become political. To achieve this, it only took writing some slogan or other on a few pieces of paper against the regime and tossing them about in the dining room in front of the guards. This "career change" always succeeded. The communist authorities exploited this rabble shamefully. There was no misdemeanor, villainy or crime that he would hesitate to perform.

My neighbor in solitary had accumulated so much bitterness and hatred that he was prepared to stand alone with knife in hand against the whole world, believing that he would be victorious. He was capable of detonating, annihilating, derailing trains… What, children? After all, these were the pioneers, the flowers of communism! His loathing was intense and he was prepared to do anything. Let the world drop dead!

Nevertheless, my neighbor excelled in deep knowledge and his speech was fluent. He was eager to enrich his world. He asked me enthusiastically about the Jews. Such a refined intelligent being, this nice Russian lad. In farewell, he dedicated his flustered poem and read it to me. Thinker, politician, psychologist, poet, Christian. A burning soul: pure heart, tragic destiny, penetrating thought. I wouldn't be hearing his voice again soon. And when I did hear it—the tables had been turned.

The Guards Spoke Russian

After solitary, I was dizzied by the circle of punishment: commands, harsh regimes of malnutrition, the blurred rotation of cells. The prison filled up with the participants in the camps' resistance movements. This rising tide swept all kinds of people into it.

One of them had become intolerable in the cell, like many of my camp companions. There was a simple reason for this intolerance. In the camp you had contact with him several minutes a day, but in the prison—24 hours a day. His name was Alex. He was a difficult man, who saw plots and intrigues everywhere. He was suspicious of everyone, as the reverse was true. He was an inexhaustible source of conflict. He had been a worker, liked uninhibited entertainments, and was a sworn fisherman. Once, while still a free man, he wasn't given time off from work during fishing season. As a result he wrote on his ballot everything that he thought about the authorities. His ballot was taken from the voting box, Alex was identified, arrested, and received his five years. In the frozen solitary cells of the camps he had become disabled: he became sick with a severe ear disease. They operated on his ear, but nothing helped. Alex became deaf.

His deafness heightened his suspiciousness because he didn't hear what was being talked about by his cellmates. He assumed they were talking about him critically. However, the real intrigues took place outside the cell. They inserted arsenic into a hole in one of Alex's teeth, and "forgot" to remove it. We raised a scandal and the guards, who feared exposure, reacted quickly this time. Alex told about how the big-figured "nurse" had treated him efficiently. She was just his type. He didn't hold anything back and during the treatment, he lightly pressed up against her thick body ... we chuckled at this description of the "nurse": "You know that you hugged the honorable chief doctor Butova in person?!"

They had mutilated Alex for five years, as they were mutilating Gunnar Rodeh for fifteen years. It had begun before his arrest. The KGB feared that Gunnar had already sensed the detectives on his trail. The KGB knew that this biologist, one of Latvia's star athletes, could manage in the forest as if he were right at home. Under the pretext that one of "their" doctors was providing treatment, they destroyed half of his teeth. With teeth like that, he wouldn't be able to survive in the forest!

Jacob and the cannibal

Afterward, Gunnar was arrested for the crime of belonging to a nationalist group that dreamed of restoring Latvia's independence. Furthermore, during his fifteen-year prison sentence, he was at Vladimir twice. They also had "forgotten" arsenic in his tooth until his entire body was poisoned, turned blue, began to give off a sharp smell of garlic and stopped functioning. Gunnar Rodeh had again been on the verge of death during his prior imprisonment at Vladimir. Real animals ruled at the top of the half-criminal prisoners at that time. Altercations erupted over every bit of nonsense, and metal bowls flew about in the air like mortar shells. A new prisoner was examined from head to foot with much consideration: in which direction were the heels of his shoes worn out, how were his earlobes attached. According to these "reliable" signs, they would decide the fateful question: Was he a Jew?

Once, one of the half-criminals fought with Sukharieva (who was the assistant of Butova, the director of the prison's medical department). The frisky witch decided to take revenge. She mixed a sexually stimulating substance with glucose, and aided by a nurse, she directed this explosive substance to the prisoner's cell. Let him go crazy! The prisoners were most surprised by the generous offer to partake of the glucose. It hadn't been possible to obtain glucose by any means, and suddenly, here Sukharieva was offering it to them on her own initiative! There's a common saying in Russia: "If they give you—take; if they hit you—run!" All the more so in prison. They took it, they tasted it. However, Sukharieva had overdone it, and this overdose didn't stimulate them sexually, but caused contractions. All of the glucose eaters bent over and grabbed their stomachs: the spasms were tormenting.

All the prisoners gradually recovered, but Gunnar, who was small-bodied, had eaten more than the others and continued entire nights bent over on his bed, moaning in excruciating pain. The doctors didn't pay any attention to him, until the half-criminals wrote a petition that Gunnar had apparently gone mad. He was taken to the cell for the insane. He begged for a doctor's visit, but to no avail. Ultimately, they arranged a meeting with a psychiatrist.

"So, what are we complaining about?" the psychiatrist asked

The Guards Spoke Russian

with a small, typical smile. When he saw Gunnar's stomach, his smile turned into an expression of terror in a split second.

"Sit, sit quietly!" the nurse began to shout and left the cell, running to bring a surgeon. It was as if a fist stuck out of Gunnar's stomach. His intestines had become twisted. This case had been extraordinarily neglected. Gunnar woke up in the midst of the operation, fully conscious that he was dying. He stood up, wanting to hurl a last curse at Moscow, but fell back unconscious. His body trembled from electric shock. The doctors activated his heart which had gone silent. Burn marks remained on his arms from the electrodes. This young sportsman, who had so recently radiated vitality, now looked like an old, sickly person. Only his spirit remained young and full of life. For his crime of refusing to take part in slave labor, he was put in the punishment cell of the camp where he became ill with scurvy, a disease caused by severe lack of vitamins which caused, among other things, tooth loss and the rotting of the living body.

While in the cell, Gunnar took a map, and guided us with his finger: here was the habitation of the Baltic tribes. Here, he pointed to Smolensk, sat a people called Goliad. There—Yatviagim. Here—Prussians (not the Germans, but the people who had preceded them in the area). These people no longer existed.

Now all that remained were only two nationalities: the Lithuanians and the Letts. "One of these two peoples is already dying," he said and circled his homeland, Latvia, with his finger. The number of invaders had already reached that of the native population. The Letts were approaching the situation of being a national minority within their own country! It had already become difficult to hear the Latvian language within Riga, the capital city. Residents of entire neighborhoods had been thrown in trains and transferred to Siberia; the invaders sat in their place. Many had been murdered. Many had been tortured to death. The death rate for Letts had outpaced the births: the Latvian people had refused to bring slaves into the world. Indeed, until recently they had been an independent people, a member country of the League of Nations (the former incarnation of the United Nations). "My God, save Latvia!" was the prayer of the nation's loyalists, chiseled on the planks in solitary.

Jacob and the cannibal

Perhaps because of his people's miserable condition, Gunnar had occupied himself as a scientist in a program to save extinct species. This was a consolidated, multi-level program and its findings had remained imprisoned and sealed. Not only did the individual need to be erased, but also his work. It didn't matter what field he had engaged in or what benefit could come from his ideas. An all-encompassing and absolute ban. Choking spirit and thought along with torturing the body.

On one of the October nights in 1975, while I was in ward 4 and Gunnar was already somewhere else, we were awakened by loud shouting. The powerful voice of one of the prisoners shouted with all his might to a window in one of the adjacent cells: "Ass-faced Nurse Genady! Bring me my medicine, you damn bitch! Brezhnyeva Leonida! Bring me my medicine, you damn bitch!" In the night stillness, the clear voice permeated the prison. I knew the voice from somewhere, but couldn't remember where from.

From the side cell, the gloomy and forlorn voices of the criminals arose: "Don't disturb our sleep..." and "Hey, you, scoundrel, do you feel like it or what? So, why don't you say something? Cat got your tongue?"

And again from somewhere in the frozen silence, calls of protest for the day of the revolution: "Invaders from the Middle East! Get out of Holy Mother Russia!"

"Orthodox Christians! Let's set out on a crusade to Jerusalem to free the grave of the son of our God from the hands of the heretics and let's punish the kikes who sold Jesus and let's avenge the blood of our king and emperor and the members of his family who were slaughtered for no reason! Long live the city of eternal youth, Kiev, the capital of the holy Russian empire!"

Night, silence, dark, everything dormant; only that concealed voice filling the universe with mysterious terror. All of a sudden I knew who it was! It was my "noble" friend from the neighboring solitary cell, the "new Noah!"

Another voice rose, suddenly, distant, fragmented: "The political prisoner Gunnar Rodeh is dying! He needs an operation urgently!"

Gunnar again had begun to experience excruciating pain in his stomach. His intestines had again become twisted. Since evening, his cellmates had tried to persuade the guards to give him emergency medical assistance, but they were ignored. In the small hours of the night, Gunnar was at risk of dying. He passed out from the pain. His cellmates tore out the bench and broke the food window in the cell door with it. Only then was Gunnar taken to the prison hospital, and thus his life was saved. The friends who had helped him were thrown into solitary. Among them was the renowned Vladimir Bukovsky.

Ultimately, the "new Noah" found out that I was sitting in the cell next to his. As if nothing had happened, he sent me a friendly note. He hoped that I hadn't identified him by his voice.

Later on, something similar happened to Jacob. Upon returning from solitary, he told us in amazement about the man in the solitary cell next to his. According to the story, he had ended up in the criminal prisoners' camp because of something trivial while a child.

A capo, who was a scoundrel and an informer who oversaw the tree cutting in the forest, harassed the youth, sought him out, and made his life bitter. The young man had had enough and decided to die. Before that, he would kill the scoundrel to avenge the prisoners who had died because of him. The other prisoners pitied the lad, distanced him, and killed the capo themselves with their axes. They faced a firing squad for that. That's when he had been inspired: why protect his miserable life which anyway was in constant danger? If he had to live, so then let it be with honor, and if to die, let that be with honor too. Since that day, he stopped having compassion for every informer and capo, as well as for himself. He became a knight of justice who had sentenced himself to life imprisonment. Every trivial occurrence lengthened his sentence; he would never leave the camps and prisons. However, he was happy because he knew why he was living.

"That's a man!" Jacob said in awe.

Once, when we were in contact passing information through the criminals' cell, I asked where Jacob's friend was sitting. "The cannibal, huh?"

"What do you mean, cannibal?!"

"And what a cannibal! He escaped from the camp, taking a

young prisoner with him, fat and appetite-arousing, who of course didn't guess why he had merited the honor. As the food ran out, he ate him, bones and all! That was his food stock. Two-legged food! Everyone knows this. He was caught, judged, he got a lengthy sentence. What do you have to do with him?"

Poor Jacob held his peace. There was something symbolic about his shameful awe of the man. The smell of history and the flavor of our period came from it.

The dam burst

Sometimes I received evidence of the use of chemical substances that strongly influenced a person's spirit and overall condition. These substances were secretly introduced into the food. Their use was particularly callous and was most common in the Ukraine. Here is some of the evidence.

Oles Sergyenko was arrested in Kiev in 1972, accused of nationalism. In the KGB's jail, after having eaten the food he was given, he felt a lowering of his mood; he became very depressed and felt pain and limpness throughout his entire body, as if suffering from some mysterious illness. When he arrived at our camp, I discerned a prominent bald spot on his chin. He explained that was something new, the result of the use of chemical substances. There was no doubt there were traces remaining inside his body that were no less horrible. He had become quite a sick individual.

Anatoly Zdorovy had been arrested in Kharkhov in 1972 or in 1973. He also had been accused of Ukrainian nationalism. His "crime" also had been an ideological one. "It would have been better to have murdered someone!" shouted the interrogator.

Zdorovy was a scientist and he was very cool-tempered. Therefore it wasn't difficult for him to detect sudden changes and extreme emotional states. When he returned to his cell from the interrogation, he noticed that there were strange green streaks in the butter which had been sent to him by his relatives. He ignored it, ate, and felt the most unusual effect to his mood. Zdorovy was certain that the KGB had up to thirty chemical substances which caused a whole spectrum of exceptional states, from euphoria to uncontrollable urges to cry like a baby. The total artificiality of these states was evident, but it was difficult to cope with them.

These substances were used overtly when dealing with spies, not as a secret additive to food. Vladimir Konstantinovsky had been arrested October 30, 1973, accused of collaborating with British intelligence. After he had been brutally beaten, he was injected with chemical substances which had three different types of influence: 1. Severe head pain. A sensation as if the brain was being pierced by white-hot needles and the head was being sawed. 2. Intense pain in all the joints as if they were being broken. 3. Weakness, apathy, sleeplessness. The injections were given openly as part of the torture.

Roman Haiduk was arrested March 23, 1974, for the crime of distributing Ukrainian publications which hadn't received the authorities' permission. He was interrogated in the KGB's Ivanofrankivsk Prison (Kolomyia). The name of his interrogator was Andrusiv.

"It won't work!" Haidok cut off the interrogation right at the start.

"It will work! We've broken tougher ones than you!"

"It doesn't matter, my skin's thick enough."

"It will burst!"

However, neither interrogation nor informers in the cells managed to break Haiduk's spirit. Then, he began to detect that something wasn't quite right about him: strong pains in his shins. It required extra effort in the interrogation not to respond to the interrogator's questions. In the cell, he looked in a small mirror and saw that his pupils were dilated. Nothing like that had ever happened to him before. His cellmate, an informer, asked him slyly: "My shin hurts. How about yours?"

"Mine doesn't," Haiduk responded. He understood that he was the victim of a substance that damaged psychological inhibition. He began to look attentively at his cellmate's behavior. The latter only ate the potatoes from the soup and dumped out the liquid. Haiduk began to do likewise. Gradually his body regained strength and all the unusual phenomena disappeared.

The two-month arrest period for interrogation had ended and the interrogation had not progressed. An expert from the KGB arrived. Haiduk answered him in such a sophisticated manner that it was impossible to prove his guilt in subverting the foundation of the Soviet regime. The expert promised Haidok that he would shortly be released. The KGB went wild: What, release a detainee? Simply release him from the KGB's clutches? Then who will fear us? No, no way! Immediately, strong steps were taken.

A psychiatric examination was set for the end of May. On May 22, his cellmates were changed. Instead of one KGB agent, they introduced two new ones (later on, a third one joined them). That same day, they allowed Haiduk to receive a food package from home.

The next day, he took two teaspoons of sugar from the package and stirred them in his tea. The result was soon to follow. He had a total mental breakdown. Everything drifted. It seemed to Haiduk that he was flying somewhere or climbing the walls. He barely managed to fall into bed, held on to its metal bars with force, fastened his fingers around them, and tried with all his might not to hallucinate.

His agent-cellmates rejoiced. They grabbed their metal cups and spoons and began to drum on them saying: "Fly to the Dnieper!"

Only later did Haiduk understand the meaning of the words, but at that moment, that's not what preoccupied him. Every sound fell on his head like the blow of a sledgehammer, piercing his brain with unbearable pain. The agents knew how they should operate.

What saved this man? Only his extraordinary strength, both mental and physical, as if he was cast out of solid iron. Haiduk barely remembered his name in the morning. He concentrated all his strength to oppose the enforced madness. It also turned out that the grams of sugar belonging to the prison food ration had contained something "extra." After ingesting them, Haiduk saw an intense, green line with rough ends when he closed his eyes. He decided not to touch any food except for bread and water from the faucet.

One of the agents whispered to his colleague: "He must be put in a cell without a faucet!"

The Guards Spoke Russian

Haiduk heard but pretended that he hadn't. On the walk, the agents moved about in a unified group. One of them instructed the others in a whisper: "The investigators don't have enough material for a trial; therefore he has to be sent to Dniepro."

Haiduk understood that they were talking about the terrible psychiatric institute in Dniepropetrovsk. Everyone—the agents in the cell, the prison administration, and the KGB agents—actively pressured him to eat everything they gave him. Haiduk offered the agents to eat the contents of the package he had received. They laughed and refused: "Eat it yourself!" they said.

In the pauses between interrogations, the KGB agents gave him a rich lunch, over which floated the light scent of a pharmacy. Haiduk secretly poured it into a bucket:

"So, you liked the borshch?" one of the interrogators asked tensely.

"Yes, very much!"

"Good, now it will work!" Andrusiv was happy. At the conclusion of the interrogation, he shook his head in disappointment: "You are a difficult man…"

They interrogated him about the names and addresses of his relatives and their life histories. There was no practical connection between this and his investigation. No secrets were hidden, everything was open and known: the interrogators examined how far his memory had been destroyed. Haiduk made an effort and remembered everything. In the prison corridors, in the yard, in the entryway, psychiatrists in civilian clothing observed him. They adopted odd exercises in order to test his response to sudden stimuli. His exceptional mental fortitude was victorious. He was recognized as sane thanks to his stubborn refusal to eat "processed" food.

Another kind of pressure was exerted on Haiduk—"a straitjacket." At the end of the investigation, a new informer began to create provocations. No evasive maneuvers helped. The guards attacked Haiduk, shackled him, dragged him to the basement and dressed him in a special shirt made from a material that shrank when wet. This shirt strangled his chest like a snake and cut off breathing, resulting in loss of consciousness. Despite this, Haiduk was not broken.

The dam burst

"So what? Has my skin burst?" Haiduk asked the interrogator Andrusiv who lowered his head and was silent.

Haiduk considered his five years of imprisonment as a victory. Moreover—as a salvation. He had undergone all the abuse of Camp 36 and was sent to Vladimir Prison for becoming a political prisoner (the refusal to serve as a slave in the camp factory). He considered all of these minor in contrast to the threat to his sanity, which he had overcome miraculously despite the pressure of the interrogation.

The question comes up here: how many people hadn't overcome and therefore had remained anonymous? How many people whose minds had intentionally been destroyed had been thrown into closed psychiatric institutions?

The ideological scale of values has a decisive weight in this matter too. If the regime is paradise on earth, only an insane, disturbed person would not love it. The solution originated with this.

I was slightly acquainted with the political prisoner Grigory Prikhodko. He was an officer. He was sent from the Ural camps to Vladimir for the crime of active participation in resistance. In my cell, information was received from him about his time in the special psychiatric institution Serbsky. Prikhodko related that since the fall of 1973, they had begun to add a special substance to the food in that hospital. As a result, Prikhodko no longer understood anything in the books he read. Limpness also appeared, as well as a tendency to sleep. None of which was normal. Prikhodko decided to withstand this situation. He chose a particularly difficult book by Hegel and by exercising all his will, he decided to break through to the meaning of the sentences. Gradually, he began to understand what he was reading but at the price of severe headaches, which have sometimes persisted to the present day.

The syndrome described here was identical to what I had felt in the autumn of 1972 in the punishment cell at Camp 36. There were three of us in the cell: me, Berezin and Grigoriev. The cabbage soup we had received for lunch was disgusting. There was something odd about it, a bland and foul taste, and unnatural color. The cabbage looked as if it was in the process of decomposing because of something chemical. The three of us felt the same symptoms that Prikhodko had described. We talked about it and were surprised that the three of us had the exact same symptoms, understanding that something had been added to the soup. I stopped eating it. Despite my hunger, I couldn't put it in my mouth.

We created a scandal, and announced it to the entire camp. The Bolsheviks were horrified. Although they didn't send our complaints anywhere, they replaced the cabbage soup with something more edible. By their alarmed reaction, there must have been something to it. Should the campaign be crowned with success, I would appear in the camp with an expression of stupidity on my face. Even my friends wouldn't have suspected anything. It may certainly be that a person can lose his mind in jail.

One day, Zdorovy was called to the office of the punishment cells at Camp 36 for a medical exam. When Dr. Petrov (the KGB coordinator as we later learned) entered, his glance encountered a dresser where there was a cup with a pinkish liquid.

"Why is this cup here?" Petrov shouted with hysterical agitation. The two most loyal guards, Mekhnotin and Rotenko were dumbstruck. Petrov pounced on the cup, hid it with his body and removed it from the office. Zdorovy understood that it was the solution that had been added to the food.

Valentin Moroz had undergone a double series of tortures: destruction of his spirit and living in the company of the craziest recruited criminal prisoners who made his life hell even by Vladimir Prison standards. They beat him, cut him with a knife, tried to destroy him by homosexual means. He preferred to sit in solitary and the punishment cell in solitary, but that eased the work of destroying his spirit.

"I would stick something into your vein to remove you from this situation," the KGB psychiatrist, Rogov, would say to him with "compassion." Moroz, therefore, declared a prolonged hunger strike. Then he underwent the third torture: forced feeding, through a tube which was intentionally wide, so that it nearly tore his esophagus.

Vladimir Balakhobov, a diplomat deserter, had experienced

interrogation in psychiatric institutions whose role was to destroy the spirit. For a long time afterward, in the camp, he was afraid to eat.

Vladimir Krasniak had become an guinea pig in prison. Gennady, Butova's son, beat the soles of Krasniak's feet with a wooden mallet and demanded that he agree to all sorts of injections. One kind of injection would have nearly turned him into a vegetable, and another kind caused him to climb the walls and bite the bars.

In the perception of the communist government (if the government is in their hands, of course), nothing was off-limits in experiments with human beings. On the contrary, they were cheaper than animals (they're obtained for free) and it was easier to hunt them down. Similarly, the experiment was direct and real. There was no need to translate the effect of the substance on the experimental animal into its hypothetical effect on a human. In their eyes, Mengele merely belonged to a rival system. His deeds weren't deviant in their eyes.

Helena Botova engaged in mass experiments on the prisoners. It seems that she examined new drugs in coordination with the Soviet health system as well as biological means of warfare. Ogurtsov was once dissuaded from drinking boiled water by something from the cell's container, water that was distributed to everyone. The rest of the cell's prisoners drank the water. The prison soon thundered with the sound of fists pounding on the cells' iron doors. Terrible diarrhea, reminiscent of dysentery, raged through the prison. Anyone who had drunk the boiled water the previous night (and there were many) had diarrhea. They were not allowed to go to the bathroom. The prisoners spread newspaper on the floor and defecated there. They were all taken to the bathroom the next morning.

Ogurtsov wrote a complaint to the Soviet Red Cross. Generally, prisoners' complaints weren't worth the paper they were written on, but in this instance, Butova suddenly got worried, called Ogurtsov in for a talk and insisted that he not send his complaint. In exchange, Ogurtsov demanded that she tell him what all that had been about and he promised to keep it secret.

The Guards Spoke Russian

"That's too much!" Butova was furious.

Many times, the prisoners used to shatter the glass panes in the prison and shout in a chorus through the bars in the direction of the city: "The communists are poisoning us!"

I was a witness to the attempts of the "doctors" to poison Ogurtsov with arsenic in the routine, overt, and arrogant manner. In early 1974, the dentist decided to take care of a hole in one of his teeth. First the nerve had to be killed and to do that it was customary to insert cotton wool with arsenic into the hole for a day.

"Tomorrow, you'll take it out?" Ogurtsov asked the nurse.

"Yes, yes, of course!" the dark, fat nurse with the slanted eyes responded.

A day and a half went by. We pounded on the door, demanded, reminded—it was no use! The same the next day. And on the third day. For several days we each pounded, taking turns, on the door; we reminded the nurse and the person in charge of the ward; we demanded that a doctor be brought in or the on-duty officer. We demanded a metal hook so that we could try to extract the arsenic by ourselves, but to no avail. It was as if talking to a brick wall. It was clear that this was a conspiracy. The tooth was already lost. It had disintegrated, but the arsenic had begun to infiltrate his body through the nerve. We had already learned about this from Gunnar Rodeh, whose tooth had also disintegrated and who had also been poisoned in a critical, near-fatal manner.

The first signs of poisoning had begun for Ogurtsov. We decided to declare a hunger strike. I also promised to reveal this barbaric crime. Only then was the arsenic removed.

It shouldn't be forgotten that the KGB doctors' destructive activities were executed upon a fertile and well-fertilized backdrop of vitamin deficiency, prolonged starvation, scurvy, and many other negative factors which were well organized. Zdorovy, for example, had been hospitalized in prison because of joints that had swelled due to hunger and pneumonia due to the cold. He was not an exception. It was routine.

Soviet Russia's law had never been like the law of other nations. A Nazi camp commander was on the wanted list his entire life in many countries, but a Siberian camp commander, who had perhaps killed as many human beings, was never on a wanted list anywhere. It was possible to sanction Libya until it gave up its perpetrators of crimes; but aid rained down on Russia in tens of billions without anyone demanding that it return Wallenberg alive or dead or that it extradite the organizers of Kennedy's assassination. Everything was permissible for Russia. It was impossible to prosecute either those who brought down the Korean plane or an outstanding hangman from the cellars of the KGB. As serious as a crime might be, it was not a crime in the eyes of the moralists and defenders of humanity if it had been executed in the service of Soviet Russia. That is food for thought.

Here is the place to also remember something relating to the devotees of "Big Brother," the warriors for rights outside the Iron Curtain, those knights of morality and the spirit who indeed belatedly got rid of the pictures of the "rising sun" from the dining rooms, but who never opposed the development of close relationships with the satanic regime. The opposite was true. They were prepared to ingratiate themselves in order to receive Russia's hug. How many curses, and embargos, and how much ostracism poured down upon the regimes of Chile or South Africa, which were relatively benign compared to the regime of "the second homeland!" Until today, the last nature preserve on earth where Soviet songs symbolizing the period are sadly and nostalgically broadcast. These include marching songs of the camp guards in precise translation to Hebrew. Those who sing these songs have no idea that the red commissar they are singing about with enthusiasm is comparable to the murderers of another dark regime.

The whirlpool of terror

No one knew how deep the terrors would go. The story of a criminal prisoner named Rakhman illuminated the depths with a murky light.

The Guards Spoke Russian

These events occurred in the first half of the 1950s. Rakhman stayed in Kazan Prison; afterward in camps for criminal prisoners. The cells were full to the brim. Conditions were terrible, the exploitation was severe. In the absence of medical assistance, the brutality and arbitrariness of the regime was obvious. However, hunger overshadowed all of that. Rakhman began to speak with trusted companions about a strike which indeed soon broke out with surprising unity. The guards were helpless. The area prosecutor arrived. Edible food appeared in the dining room. Many were hospitalized. Seemingly, it was a smashing victory. Later on, all the activists were suddenly taken on a journey.

"Where are we being taken? To trial?" the camp activists wondered.

The "crow" brought them to some airfield. They were loaded onto a plane. What could it be? No one understood. The deserted expanse of Tataria sprawled under the wings of the plane.

The plane landed on a godforsaken landing strip. Again, the "crow"; everyone shackled. A stop. The rattling of iron. The "crow" entered somewhere. Judging by the echo, it was a closed structure. Rattling again. A reverberation like that in a garage. The prisoners were taken out of the "crow" into a strange, closed structure.

Rakhman was led to an opening in the floor where written in white was: "00" (in discussion we have concluded that "00" in an accepted Soviet code meant "top secret"). The round door covered in a soft material opened noiselessly. Guards in blue jackets and soft shoes led him downstairs. A corridor, artificial lighting. On both sides rows of sealed openings with the same mysterious double zeroes. Everything was silent. Where next? Another opening in the floor. More stairs. Another floor below. An identical corridor, the same figures walking silently in blue jackets and soft shoes. One more floor, down again. How many identical subterranean floors were there? How far underground was he? Finally, a round door was soundlessly locked behind his back. A narrow cell, its length slightly more than a person's height. In the middle, something covered in wood protruded, apparently something to lie down upon. On the side there was a shallow depression made of concrete. Was that for toileting needs? But it had no outlet!

The whirlpool of terror

Aside from this, the cell had nothing else in it. Was it solitary confinement? He was forced to urinate in the concrete depression. There was nowhere else. He began to bang on the round opening, but the sound was barely audible. He shouted with all his might. He became tired. Suddenly the round door opened.

"What's the matter?" asked a figure in a blue jacket.

"I need to wash myself... I'm hungry...."

"There's no bathing here!" and the door locked silently. He was alone again. Rakhman lay down on the narrow surface, near his urine. The walls were made out of a special substance, which was smooth and hard. It was impossible to scratch it or climb it. Dim light shone down from the ceiling. Through an opening in it, hot or cold air alternately flowed into the cell.

Rakhman was terrified. He had once heard off-handedly from religious prisoners about a terrifying, underground prison, Chistopol "double zeroes." The story had sounded for him like a fable.

No one came back from there, he was told. What would become of him now? Would they test out biological warfare methods on him? Chemical ones? What did those mysterious white zeroes mean on the burgundy-colored round openings? Why was it so deadly silent? He had no answers. Worn out, he fell into a deep sleep. When he woke up, he didn't know how much time had passed, whether it was morning or evening. He saw a blue figure in the opening, a man of middle-age, his eyes and cheeks deeply sunken, with two others next to him, ordinary supervisors.

"Do you have any questions?" the middle-aged man asked in a tough, sharp tone.

"What crime have I been placed in this solitary for? Where am I? No one informed me about punishment! What am I accused of?"

The middle-aged man's facial expression changed from a slight smile of understanding to something like sorrow.

"You're here for having been brought here! You'll get food once a day. Once a day you can ask for water. To do this you have to approach the opening and make a sound. For toileting—there," he said and pointed to the depression in the floor. "Once a day they'll bring you a vessel and a scoop, and you have to scoop. That's all. In fifteen or thirty days, depending on your conduct, maybe you'll be moved to a cell with more comfortable conditions. Pay attention, this is for your own good! You are staying here for having been brought here. Internalize this," he ended emphatically.

The door was locked. They brought a piece of black bread. For a whole day. Rakhman, who was hungry, swallowed it in one gulp and wasn't full. He lay down; recumbent, he nearly filled the entire cell's length and width. From above the same wind blew: sometimes hot, sometimes cold. Rakhman was determined not to surrender. For the first time in his life, he declared a hunger strike, preferring to die and not to fall victim to secret experiments or to be driven insane from this absolute solitude. He lay for several days without moving, without paying attention to anything, without eating. He noted the days that went by only by the opening, which opened and closed immediately without a sound. Two weeks later, a doctor in a white jacket appeared, to artificially feed him.

Rakhman continued his hunger strike. As if in a dream, the face of a silver-haired guard once bent over him.

"Listen to me," an elderly voice said. "I've served here dozens of years already. My hair turned white from this work, but as far as I can remember, no one has left here alive. Did you ever hear of 'double zero' Chistopol Prison?!"

Again the door locked. Only the last mysterious and threatening sentence remained hanging in the air.

He was taken very infrequently in a special cart for bathing. Mute slaves, apparently prisoners like him, silently turned his body around under the shower. Afterward, the cart returned to the same opening. They laid Rakhman down in his place, the opening soundlessly locked. The hunger strike went on for nearly 180 days and Rakhman was victorious. When he was already half-dead, they took him from the underground prison to the Kazan psychiatric institution. A new journey through circles of hell began there: wandering among psychiatric institutions.

Rakhman returned "to his circles" only after many years and then was taken to "regular" places of imprisonment. His term of imprisonment was essentially infinite. Occasionally suspicious persons (prisoner collaborators) attacked him on transfers, in cells, and tried to murder him. However, each time he was saved by a miracle. On his journey to Vladimir, he managed to get a knife out of an assailant's hand and stab him. His term was lengthened again and again. Here in Vladimir, they created the same atmosphere for him. He was often sent to solitary. He suffered from a serious disease. It was clear that he was living on borrowed time. However, he didn't want to take his secret to the grave. Thus he used an opportunity to tell about the underground prison to the political prisoner who crossed his path.

Gog and Magog

During the period of my last imprisonment, a new spirit emerged. Several Russians also began to spring up in the camps, unswerving democrats, members of the democratic movement. The KGB reacted as usual. Yegor Davidov, who had been arrested for the crime of distributing the democratic movement's literature, related what had happened to him in the KGB's detention center in Leningrad.

A criminal prisoner suddenly appeared in his cell. He had been brought from one of the camps for no reason. In the middle of Yegor's interrogation, the criminal began to threaten him, saying that he would poke out his eyes, and described in great detail how he would do this. The authorities did things like that so that the detainees would be afraid of even going to sleep. The purpose was to get the prisoner off-balance emotionally, to destabilize his nervous system, and ultimately break him down. Yegor didn't submit to this terror, despite the threats.

Generally, the prison psychiatrist, Rogov, harassed the prisoners at his own initiative. However, I requested permission for a meeting with him and before I left the prison, although with much difficulty, they permitted this meeting.

It turned out that the notorious spider was a smiling, young man, quiet as a cat, with hypnotic, glittering brown eyes. The essence of his outlook was that we were all simple mortals. Due to our being ignorant of psychiatry, we had no right to interfere with the deeds of the omnipotent and all-knowing priests of psychiatry. They alone were licensed to decide who among the mortals would be left alone and who would be imprisoned forever in the "sanatorium"—essentially a prison for torture and destruction of the spirit.

"A person can appear totally normal, but only we, the experts, see at first glance that he is insane," Rogov declaimed for me to hear.

So simple! There was no need for investigation, judges, and sentences. The holy and infallible psychiatric inquisition which didn't have to account for its deeds to anyone except the KGB was sufficient, and it was all in the name of science!

I asked to know if Rogov acknowledged the relationship between the patient's physical condition and mental condition.

"Why do you ask me the questions of a student?" Rogov was insulted.

"Because none of the many starving prisoners that you've 'diagnosed' has received a diet prescribed by you to bolster them, something which a regular doctor sometimes prescribes! You never gave anyone vitamins, the lack of which destroys the body and the mind! Or do you only use hunger as preventive medicine?"

"You're not an expert, not an expert, not an expert!" Rogov shouted hysterically, as if a recording was stuck in his throat.

"Perhaps explain to me what psychiatric principle makes prisoners 'sick' only at the end of their prison term, and not when it's started or in the middle?"

"That's not correct. Look at Yatsishin, for example," Rogov responded agitatedly.

"You didn't diagnose Yatsishin as mentally ill. We forced you to recognize him as such, forcibly! Tell me the name of one political prisoner, who you, at your initiative, sent for treatment not at the end of his prison term, but at the beginning or in the middle!"

I counted the names of several dozen prisoners who had been "diagnosed" as mentally ill only at the end of their prison terms at Vladimir. Thus, instead of the release which they so anticipated, they were given a new prison sentence, a psychiatric one, with no final date.

Rogov was forced to admit that this "principle" did not apply to criminal prisoners. The psychiatrist felt such pressure that his body began to tremble when I started to speak about Moroz and Lukiyanenko, hunger strikers for whom Rogov had invested exceptional effort to have transferred to a psychiatric hospital. He completely refused to talk with me about those two individuals.

Lukiyanenko's story was particularly representative. He was held for fifteen years (after he had been sentenced to death), only because he had expressed the idea of Ukrainian secession from the Soviet Union. Lukiyanenko was a native of Chernigov which had "enjoyed" hundreds of wonderful years under the yoke of Moscow. He had been imprisoned twice in Vladimir. During his first incarceration, he had almost died from poisoning. The Bolsheviks had added something to his food. Only after a number of years, when Lukiyanenko was imprisoned in Vladimir because of opposition he demonstrated in the camp, and when his general term of imprisonment was coming to an end, only then was Rogov moved on the basis of that old complaint to a psychiatric hospital. They diagnosed him there with "hypochondria." He was classified as mentally ill, with a second degree disability. This allowed the authorities to arrest him after his "release" on the excuse that the disease had "reawakened." Lukiyanenko decided to exploit this diagnosis. Upon his return to Chernigov, his city of birth, he demanded disability benefits.

It turned out that the authorities hadn't been mistaken. This "disability" did not justify benefits according to the "law!" The KGB could only use it for purposes of arrest.

Toward the end of my stay in Vladimir, I encountered a new figure: Ugodin, an officer for special matters. He was brought in to "reinforce" because information leaking from within the prison had reached scandalous proportions. After my release, this officer became the prison commander. His activities were unique in that he decided not to release any papers out of the prison, not even those that had already passed through censorship. Beginning with the 25th Congress of the Soviet Communist Party, in the

The Guards Spoke Russian

mid–1970s, all prisoner correspondence was automatically confiscated with no explanation. The Congress was over, but the situation hadn't changed. Complaints received equal attention. All formal complaints were cancelled. In the best case scenario, Ugodin responded personally (orally) to complaints sent to any of the authorities.

Even in the instance of a complaint which had real evidence accompanying it (a fat worm pulled out of the thin mixture that was called soup), there was no response. Attention was not paid either to the petition or to the accompanying worm.

During that same period, I heard the story of a soldier who had taken part in the Yom Kippur War. His name can't be publicized out of concern for his personal safety. An entire Soviet army (approximately 50,000 soldiers) was secretly moved to Syria before the war. The transport took place by the "civilian" Soviet navy, which carried out, so it seems, not only tasks of espionage. The soldiers were put on the lower decks of fishing boats and were transported the entire way in utter, stifling darkness, like animals, without being told what their final destination was. It was forbidden to go up on the deck. The worried cannon fodder discussed the question in the ship's belly of where they were being taken. To Cuba? To Vietnam? Near the unknown shore, an announcement was made to the soldiers: "The Jews are fighting the Arabs; we're on the side of the Arabs!"

Afterward, dressed in neutral uniforms and loaded onto army trucks, they were transported through the capital city to the front. The Arabs, who recognized them as their "big brothers," welcomed them by throwing stones instead of rice and candy. Caricatures were hung everywhere in which "Uncle Vanya" was seen giving a weapon to an Arab with one hand and with the other removing his possessions from his pocket.

Initially, their battery of missiles was placed behind the Golan Heights in desert territory. The soldiers wept hearing the explosive sounds of the shelling. They didn't understand why they had been brought to die here. Afterward, they were sent to supply munitions to the front. Israeli soldiers, flown secretly by helicopter, placed an ambush on the nearby hills, surrounding one of the Russian supply convoys. The Israelis succeeded in blowing up the armored vehicle leading the convoy, setting it ablaze with their first round of fire, doing the same to the rearguard vehicle. The Russian soldiers ran about in the fire trap under a barrage of heavy machine gun fire. Many shouted "Oh, mom!"; others fell in hysteria. One of the officers pulled out his pistol and shouted: "Forward, for the homeland!" and leaped toward danger.

He was immediately killed by a round of bullets. Another round shortened the life of a friend and neighbor of the narrator of those events. He died without knowing why he had been sacrificed for the interests of the Moscow slave masters. This situation was one of multiple horrors. Young men, who had been gathered and drafted by force, sons of the nationalities enslaved by Moscow, were helping to enslave another country, and died by the bullets of its defenders. The most terrible thing etched in the memory of the witness-narrator was the sight of his friend's brain as it leaked out of its skull before his very eyes.

In the past, Soviet citizens sang an official song with the words: "I do not, I do not yearn for the Turkish coast, I have no need of Africa either." Later on these words were replaced by a more abstract version: "I don't yearn for foreign suns, and I have no need of another country," because it was already the turn of the Turkish coast and Africa.

Moscow reached out to Jerusalem, the crossroads of three continents, with passion. Jerusalem was on the route to the oil-rich Persian Gulf, where, concealed on its shores, lay the key to world rule.

Many religious people among those who stayed in the camps interpreted what was written in Ezekiel about the war of Gog and Magog as indicating Moscow, whose conquering armies would find their deaths in Israel.

A violent departure

My term of imprisonment was approaching its end. They removed me from my cell ahead of time.

The Guards Spoke Russian

"To your freedom and ours!!" my friends wished me. However, instead of leaving on a trip to freedom, I was transferred for several days to the cell of ... Kronid Lubarsky, a renowned scientist and a member of the democratic opposition! Why? we both groped in the dark.

In the meantime, we rushed to tell each other all the news that we knew. It turned out that deputy colonel Ugodin wanted to profit from both sides. On the one hand, he completely stopped Kronid's correspondence from the moment the Swiss Committee for Human Rights announced that it was awarding him a prize. On the other hand, he placed people in his cell who offered to illegally pass his letters from prison "with insurance," for 30 rubles apiece. The enigma of our surprising meeting was quickly solved: the KGB hoped to find many of Kronid's documents on my person the moment I left prison.

Therefore, the first thing they did when I was moved to one of the preparatory cells for the journey at the end of March 1976, was to confiscate all papers that I had with me for "inspection": old letters which had been officially received and had passed through the prison censorship—entire packages, postcards, family pictures, envelopes legally purchased, paper, stamps. They also took books, magazines, newspapers, every piece of paper that I possessed.

I quickly became aware that they didn't intend to return anything to me. I declared a hunger strike. The guards didn't pay attention to it, and after a short time, they brought me my possessions, dragging me like a sack to the guard room for a bodily inspection. Here, they took my last pieces of paper, and afterward began to deal with my clothing. They took my jacket somewhere, and in its place threw me a dirty, worn-out vest that had belonged to someone else. They also took the receipt form for the sum of money which had been confiscated at the time of my arrest.

Afterward, in the camp, I conducted a real "paper war," arguing that my stolen possessions be returned. At first, they gave me various odd answers: once, they said that they had never taken anything away from me; they suddenly announced that everything they had taken had been confiscated as anti–Soviet propaganda (which, as aforementioned, included the letters which had been given me by the censor himself, family pictures, Soviet postage stamps, etc.). Then they announced that they had indeed taken my sentencing document away. They even promised to return it.

No official office wanted to deal with the confused theft matter. Only after I had left for "freedom," similar to house arrest, did I manage to obtain my sentencing document from them. Money, books, family pictures, jacket, stationery, letters, etc., etc. All that remained with Deputy Colonel Ugodin.

The Vladimir mafia was invincible. It operated according to the declaration of rights of an independent fortress. Even far superior authorities didn't want to interfere with its internal matters. Ugodin was a bit stupid, apathetic, and dull, with small, watery eyes which always seemed to express a question mark, and he spoke in drawn-out syllables. You could get a faster and clearer answer from a concrete pillar than you could from him.

I continued my hunger strike, lying down in one of the transit cells. The supervisor accompanied the bodily inspection with the following words: "The Jews have Purim. When they take you away from here, it will be my Purim holiday."

The time for the departure arrived. I kept up my hunger strike and persisted in reclining, because not only did they not intend to return anything to me, they had even refused to explain their actions to me. Then it was Major Kiselyov's turn. He had a square body and his face looked like it had been sculpted from coarse stone, and left unfinished. At his instruction, the guard dragged, attacked me and beat me. At the same time, Kiselyov himself was occupied with my hands and twisted them with all his might. That's how I was thrown into the car, and I fell with my face hitting someone's knees. It was a criminal prisoner stumbling from the neighboring transit cell.

"Here's their humanity, director!" he grumbled from his place and helped me to sit next to him while he held my shoulder so that I wouldn't fall because of the potholes on the road. He was a Ukrainian from Koban. It was thanks to him that I was relatively secure without having any special adventures in the company of the criminal prisoners who stumbled about throughout the journey to Kirov, on the way to the Urals.

The Guards Spoke Russian

The KGB agents had an entirely different purpose when they seated me among them. Fortunately, not all criminal prisoners were alike. One of the travelers read to his neighbors an entire philosophical treatise about his way of life, a copy of which he had sent to Suslov, the famous, last philosopher of hardline communism during Brezhnev's time. He had hoped for a pardon.

During pauses between reading passages, he told piquant and salacious stories about his life, or looked adoringly at the backside of the young guard who walked about by the cages.

My neighbor from the Kuban told me about the desperate lives of the criminal prisoners at Vladimir. Many of them couldn't imagine living without improvised knives and spikes.

When brutal guards broke into the cell, the prisoners used to pull out their ready weaponry. That was the only way to deter them. Was their walk in the yard cut short from an hour and a half to an hour? The weapons appeared again and the guards were forced to continue the walk.

In the "crow" I also met Kostya Stogov, who traveled with us for a distance. He was dressed in the striped shirt of the dangerous criminals, but was not at all like the habitual prisoners. He was dark-skinned, his hair was black; in appearance, he was reminiscent of Pasternak, with his sad eyes and full lips. This young and simple man, in spite of prison and camp, completely abstained from criminal slang. He was modest and advocated goodness. He had sat in prison because of some romance. Young Romeo had entered a fight to protect his girlfriend, whom someone intended to rape, as a result, he was in the camp next to Kovrov. A murder had taken place in the camp. The investigating officer hadn't found the guilty party, and decided to make quiet Kostya the scapegoat. Due to false witnesses and erasing evidence, including that of the investigator, the innocent young man had been given a lengthy sentence. Kostya Stogov's sentence was given in December 1975. He felt that his life had ended at that instant.

Later on, in the "crow" in Kirov, I began a conversation with another young man who was being taken from Archangelsk province to the prison in Balashov. He related the resurrection of

A violent departure

Stalinism in the concentration camps in the Archangelsk area where their code name was "UG." Thus, for example, with a blow of his boot to the stomach, Captain Poyeta kicked over a young man who had been sentenced for some light crime. That happened on the eve of the young man's release. The captain left him lying in the snow. The mother came to meet her released son, and was told that he had died a short time before in the camp's sick room from serious damage to his liver.

The murderer hadn't been punished. Many young, healthy individuals became disabled for the rest of their lives. The atmosphere in the concentration camps in Archangelsk province was such that the commander might strike a subordinate officer in the face during the prisoners' line-up. If that was the behavior toward officers, it was obvious that prisoners with no rights were treated like weeds to be trampled upon any which way. This general atmosphere of the camp authorities also was expressed in the treatment of the political prisoners. Thus, for example, Abankin had been thrown into solitary when he was on a hunger strike. On the fourth day, he refused to lift up his plank during the day because according to regulations, it was permissible for a hunger striker to recline during daytime hours. For this, the on-duty guard took him out to the corridor and struck him in the ribs with his huge key ring. The doctor who examined him afterward determined: bruises due to beating.

Despite this, the guard was not punished and the striking Abankin was kept in solitary for an even longer term with raised planks. Moreover, the solitary cell was painted without removing the prisoner. He was thereby sentenced to suffocate in the wet stench of the fresh paint.

Stalinist tendencies were felt in all strata of the imperialist society. It was a kind of nostalgia for the big whip. In Leningrad, one of the movie theaters showed a film in which Stalin's image appeared on the screen. The audience stood and clapped enthusiastically. One of the old women cried with excitement and joy and wiped her tears on the edge of an embroidered handkerchief. Their god had returned!

The Urals again

This time I was taken back to the camp without any extreme measures of precaution.

Several months of imprisonment remained for me, and the Bolsheviks were no longer afraid that I would escape. They were worried by something else: in their fervor for punishment, they hadn't precisely calculated the length of my imprisonment in Vladimir. It now turned out that I was being returned to the camp for some sort of short re-acquaintance. They didn't want to show me hospitality. They were too lazy to think out and execute something smart. Only the standard solution remained. The Bolsheviks again decided to show me hospitality in solitary. It was possible to talk through the primitive sewage system between the solitary cells in the camp's punishment cells.

That's how I made the acquaintance of Ashot Navasardian, a member of the Armenian nationalist party. The most famous individual in this group was Paruyir Ayrikian. For both of them, this was their second prison term. Their idea in short was expressed in the words which occasionally appeared on the walls of houses in Yerevan, the capital of Armenia: "Russians get out! Long live independent Armenia!" After their arrest, while they were still in the KGB jail in Yerevan, they declared a hunger strike in protest. The KGB agents, using the excuse of artificial feeding, began to torture them: they crushed their tongues with special pliers, causing intolerable pain. The tongue swelled and nearly filled the entire oral cavity. After the trial, during which the accused overtly argued for their country's independence, Navasardian was brought to the concentration camp in the Urals in October 1974.

While still in the train station in Yerevan, a terrible drama took place in one of the Stolypin cars. Initially, they threw all of Navasardian's possessions out the window. Afterward, Roosevelt Sahatian, the commander of the guards and the only Armenian among them, entered his cage. For no reason, he beat Navasardian and also ordered

The Urals again

A guard tower in the camp.

The Guards Spoke Russian

the others to do likewise. All together they beat Navasardian repeatedly and brutally with fists and boots. When asked why, they replied: "So that you know what a Soviet guard is!" The tortures and beatings also continued when they took him from the cell to the bathroom.

His journey from Armenia to the Urals went on for months. All that time he stayed among the criminal prisoners. During this time, the terrible signs of the beatings managed to fade and clot. At first, the pain was so intense that Ashot feared that his ribs had been broken. The conditions of the journey were impossible to describe. Lice crawled over Ashot's body.

In the camp, he declared a strike, demanding that a referendum be held in Armenia. Because of this, he was almost never out of solitary. Later on, I had the chance to know him personally. He was tall and lean, both dark and pale, and his eyes were large and fiery. His character was that of a holy man. He well understood that there was no chance at the moment, but, despite this, he sacrificed himself. He would always bear the eternal flame of the nationalist idea, even at the price of his body. Therefore, he willingly mounted the sacrificial fire. He wanted to live and die in a way that was worthy of an Armenian.

Armenia, the most ancient of the empire's enslaved lands, had a reason to be proud. It was their ancient father, according to the national legend, who had overcome the biblical Nimrod, the first tyrant in human history. Also, in the present, Armenia was the forward outpost and the sturdiest of the nationalist opposition movements. The memory of the Armenian genocide doubled its determination.

Ashot had a lot in common with Valentin Moroz when he said: "We need envoys and tortured saints!" Thus he spoke and thus he acted.

In our conversations through the sewage pipes, Ashot acquainted me with his new cellmate, Sergei Taratokhin, who, in February 1976, revealed to the prisoners that since the previous May, he had been a snitch. The first thing he uncovered was the paper-signing ceremony in this version: "I, Taratokhin Sergei Mikhailovitch, agree to cooperate with the national security council (KGB). State secrets which become known to me during this cooperation, I promise

The Urals again

to keep secret. For undercover purposes, I will use the nickname 'Andrei.'" Date and signature.

According to Sergei, he had agreed to this for purposes of espionage. He discovered important details. It seemed that the ordinary informer's job was only the lowest level in the collaborator hierarchy. It was considered a privilege for an individual to cooperate in the KGB's operations, directed toward shaping the camp's spiritual atmosphere and public opinion. It was the same outside the camps, and even abroad.

"The hatred of nations must be sown by any means, and foremost anti–Semitism," Taratokhin was taught by KGB Major Cherniak. "Conversations on anti–Semitic subjects should be initiated and encouraged at every opportunity. The lives of Jews within the camp must be made as awful as possible!"

That was the KGB's official line, not Cherniak's free choice, even though he also would have been accepted as an honorary member of the "Black Hundred." Cherniak's rage was especially great because he hadn't succeeded in getting anyone into the Jewish group. Therefore, he didn't know anything of its mood and intentions.

An additional task was to slander the best men among the camp's political prisoners. All the members of the camp's Jewish community then (Dimshitz, Mendelevitch, Zeev Zalmanson) and also Sverstiyuk, Hrinkiv, Navasardian, and Kovalyov belonged to this select group. Many diverse methods were used against this spiritual elite.

"Navasardian is about to receive a package," Cherniak told Taratokhin. "I will personally give it to him! And you will try to bring it to the camp's attention intimating that it was for a good reason that the package was given by none other than the KGB officer himself to Navasardian!"

The most interesting thing was that both camp doctors—Petrov, the old one, a limping, drug addict with shaky hands, and the new, young one, Titov—were paid agents of the KGB.

Who would have thought such a thing about the poor, drunk cripple who once in a blue moon provided me with a few vitamins past their expiration date, while scattering them on the floor with his shaking hand. It turned out that he and his colleague received

The Guards Spoke Russian

reports from the informers, gave them tasks, and provided them with gifts in order to avoid frequent, suspect summons by the officer.

As payment for informing, Taratokhin used to receive eight packs of chocolate a month; extra food packages through the sick room; a work release or a bed in the sick room according to his wish.

Major Cherniak would summon him only in the most urgent cases. Usually he tried to end the conversation as quickly as possible. Of course, in order to cover their tracks, the group of healthy informers blended in with the regular patients, especially if too big a commotion had been raised in the West because of an absence of medical care for the prisoners. Agents in white robes—apparently that was the accepted norm in the camps.

After his release, they intended to "send" Taratokhin to the University of Moscow.

While I was still in solitary, a new Ukrainian named Mikhailo Slobodiyan arrived. During his time as a policeman, he had founded an underground organization that hung nationalist flags in the street, as well as banners calling for Ukrainian independence. In the courtroom, he said: "You can kill me in your concentration camps, but you'll never succeed in killing the growing struggle of the Ukrainian people for independence. I hate and will always hate you because of your vengeance and despicableness!"

He was sentenced to 11 years imprisonment in the camps, and three more years in exile. His accusation was based on having accepted bribes. The false witnesses, who testified in the trial that they had bribed him, were neither accused nor punished, in spite of the fact that according to Soviet law, the one who offers a bribe is a real criminal just like the one who took it.

Joseph Mendelevitch received an interesting response from the authorities regarding his complaint of religious persecution. Praying aloud was forbidden in every place of incarceration according to the Soviet government regulation dating from 1918, which had interpreted it as "preaching." The response to Joseph ended with a threatening warning not to raise this subject again.

One of the most sympathetic prisoners I ever met was a young, green-eyed man, Stefan Sapeliyak. He was born in the village

The Urals again

Rosokhatch, near Chortkiv in Ternopil province, and studied in Chortkiv. He loved his people simply and naturally, perhaps like a leaf loves a tree. Since his childhood, he had heard songs about the heroic Ukrainian struggle for independence. The people did not accept official Soviet songs. In his village, there was an historic mound where Cossacks who had died in battles for the area's independence had been buried, starting in the Middle Ages. Later on, victims of the struggle for independence in the following centuries had been buried there. All the rulers—Austrians, tsars, Poles, and Germans—had tried to destroy the mound, but the people would re-build it again and again. Only the Soviets managed to do a thorough job. Each time the peasants tried to reconstruct the destroyed mound, the Bolsheviks destroyed it again. With explosives and bulldozers, they didn't leave one remnant of the mound and scattered the bones buried there to the ravens.

In revenge, a group of young people blew up a monument to the Russian soldiers that stood with their stone machine guns threateningly over the village residents. In Chortkiv, on the 55th anniversary of the declaration of Ukrainian independence, the streets were decorated with national flags and banners and the bloody red cloths of the Soviet flag were torn down wherever possible. The inhabitants welcomed the change with much enthusiasm. On the banners, the simple folk added a drawing of a pitchfork and wrote: "Muscovites, go away."

Several pilots from the military flight school located in the region requested a transfer back within Russia on the grounds that "the nationalists threaten us." An old man, who worked as a guard, was interrogated by the police as to how it was possible that next to the bath house which he was responsible for guarding, a blue and yellow flag had appeared on the flagpole instead of the red flag.

"Dear sirs, I looked in the evening and I saw your flag. So, I went to bed. In the morning, I woke up and I saw it was already our flag!" Because of "your" and "our," innocently spoken, the old man had almost been sent to prison.

"Oh, man!" the green-eyed youth, leaning childishly on my shoulder, almost choked with laughter. This poor lad had experienced very rough things in the camp. He had been beaten by the officer, Melentiayi, and a strike broke out in protest of that. The chauvinists asked to break the strike and called the opposition "Judeo-Ukrainian conspiracies." Afterward, they took Sapeliyak to the Ukraine, where the KGB tried to "re-educate him," to brainwash him, and threatened to beat him with black rubber clubs, "to set him afloat upon the waves." They held him in terrible conditions. They demanded that he "confess" to a Ukrainian woman, a tourist from abroad, that he wasn't political at all, but a "thug," and that he had never been beaten by an officer, that there had never been a strike; even that the camp had never existed.

And then, the KGB agents winked at him, we'll thank you. They took him to the riverbank, called girls over, offered to let him leave from there for his village. The next day he could write a letter declaring his contrition, and never return again to the camp. Sapeliyak refused even to get out of the car.

"Aha, so you even had business with the merchants!" thundered the voice of the KGB agent.

"With which merchants?" Stefan didn't understand.

"With the Jews, with those traitors!" the investigator said and his face twisted with hatred.

Because of the brainwashing, Stefan's blood pressure rose in an alarming manner; however, the "doctors" refused to treat him, only looking on wide-eyed and silent .

Because he hadn't agreed to "contrition," new persecutions followed him: every month, the lad was thrown into solitary; now he had been sent to Vladimir. While in solitary, he used to turn his back the moment Cherniak, the KGB officer, entered and then shouted brutally: "I'll dry you up so that you'll have to put stones in your pockets so you won't fly off in the wind!"

Three to four times a day, Sapeliyak was stripped and they searched and burrowed in his clothing. Watchfulness!

"But aren't you afraid that I'll escape?" the laughing and naked Stefan once asked the guard whose head was drowning in Stefan's underwear.

"No, after all, I'm watching you through the fly," the guard answered in total seriousness from inside the long underwear.

Toward the exodus

At the beginning of July 1976, I was suddenly removed from my workplace and taken on a transfer. While walking along, I barely managed to say good-bye to my friends. In the watch room, I met Ashot Navasardian. We tried to guess where they were taking us. Perhaps to the Perm prison? After I was examined in a particularly thorough manner, they exchanged my clothing for new clothes from the storeroom. They were so afraid of information leaking out! If they could, they would have given me a new body, a new spirit too…

Everything made out of paper, to the very last piece, was taken for examination.

In the "crow" there was a finger-width's layer of dust. Brown and suffocating, the dust penetrated my nose. For the last time, I bumped over those potholes.

After spending the night in the Perm prison, I was separated from Navasardian. We managed to find out that he was being taken to Yerevan, and I was going to Ukraine. For some reason, they transported me from Perm to Kazan prison, to a triangular cell, totally sealed off with no windows or openings. The guards left the food window open so that at least the compressed air from the corridor would enter. There was a slop bucket, but no sink. Water was worth the weight of gold. The heat was stifling. I walked about in this box half-naked. The prison was overcrowded. Several guards asked about the political prisoners, listening with understanding to talk about the struggle for national liberation. They were Tatars. This national matter was not strange to many of them.

I was taken from Kazan to Kharkhov. All of my possessions were taken into storage. I was led to the bathhouse, but wasn't given a towel.

"Manage! We'll give you a towel later!"

It was a good thing that it was summertime.

The ethnic border of Ukraine was clearly seen from the train car. At first, houses painted white poked out among the black,

The Guards Spoke Russian

neglected, wooden huts. They then increased in number, surrounded by small gardens, flowerbeds, and tended vegetable patches. Together with the soft vocal "ha" in their speech, another spirit could be sensed beyond the window, oppressed but not dead.

When I left Kharkhov prison, the guard discovered in my suitcase a Hebrew date display, which had been officially published with the authorities' permission by the Moscow synagogue. They wanted to take it away from me. I created a real commotion and after hesitating, the date display was returned to me. However, it was too soon to celebrate. Another guard unit entered the car. An albino guard looked suspiciously at my cage. "What are you, a political one?"

"Yes."

"Do an inspection! Search well!"

They again took the date display away from me. "Aha, Jews! They should hang all of them!" the guard commander shrieked with hatred.

"The Declaration of Helsinki ensures religious rights! Brezhnev signed it! Give me back my date display. It was published in the Soviet Union by authority of the ministry that takes care of this. It says so on the cover."

"And I spit on that! I have orders printed black on white: 'To be confiscated: knives, money, and literature with religious content!' Here is a brand new instruction booklet," he said and pointed at this booklet. "I obey orders and not declarations! Is that clear?"

Absolutely. The declarations are intended for the naïve West; orders with opposite content are for the guards. Doublespeak, according to Orwell. How good it is that I'll be leaving you soon.

In the Gulag I became convinced that the conquest of the world is Russia's *idée fixe* throughout history. For this, Russia need Ukraine's resources—from annexing the history of the neighboring country to turning its brave fighters into "Russians."

The goal of Russia is the liberation of humanity from everything human. From Ivan the Terrible until today, nothing fundamental has changed there.

Index

Abankin 113, 145
Afanasov 70
Afanasyev 111–113
Afghanistan 85
Africa 141
American embassy 101
Americans 26
Andrusiv 126, 128
Angola 60, 85
anti–Semitism 25, 27, 32, 36, 40, 58, 74, 105, 149
anti–Soviet propaganda 142
Arabs 140
Archangelsk 144, 145
Arctic Circle 117
Arians 28, 103
Armenia 27, 146, 148
Armenian genocide 148
Armenians 25, 59, 67–68, 77, 95, 146, 148
Avakov 97, 98–99, 104
Ayrikian, Paruyir 146

Balakhobov, Valentine 130
Balashov 144
Baltic tribes 122
Banderovtsi 43
Baranov 35
BBC 95
Belorussia 49
Belorussians 65
Berezin 129
Beria 75
Bialik 47
Bikov 98
"the Black Hundred" 36
Boguslavsky, Victor 33
Bolshevicks 46, 47, 59, 61, 101, 118, 139, 146, 151
Brezhnev, Leonid 50, 56, 72, 23
Bukovsky, Vladimir 113

Bulgakov, Michail 83
Butov Genady 123, 131
Butova Helena Nikolayevna 38, 93, 120, 131–132

Camp 19 25, 27, 32, 42, 48, 65, 67, 70, 102
Camp 35 43, 53, 70, 110, 112
Caucasus 40, 55, 77
Chechnia 55
Cheka 5, 40, 77; *see also* KGB; NKVD
Chernigov 139
Chernoglaz, David 113
Chernyak 149–150, 152
Chetin 14
Chevico, Bogdan 44
Chile 133
China 60, 85, 101–102, 108
Chinese 39, 85, 102, 108, 109
Chinese meal 108
Chistopol Prison 136
Chmelnitsky monastery 117
Chortkiv 151
Christianity 19, 35, 58, 73
Communism 54, 57–59, 62, 72, 96, 100
Communist Party 140
Comsomol 72
Cossacks 151
"crow" 69, 85, 134, 153
Cuba 140
Cubans 85
Czechoslovakia 47, 117

Dante 76
Davidov, Yegor 137
Davis, Angela 99
"The Declaration of Helsinki" 154
Dimshitz 149
Diyak, Michailo 86
Dnepropetrovsk 104, 128
"doctors plot" 55

155

The Guards Spoke Russian

East Germany 25
Engels 56
England 117
Estonians 46, 50

Fedorenko, Vasil 117
Feodorov 73–74, 78
Finland 85, 104
Furtseva, Ekaterina 72

General Bezuchov 36–37
Gerasimov 111
German police 34
Germans 26, 46, 50, 62, 115, 122
Germany 26, 117
Greece 50
Grigoriev 72, 77, 129
Guliyaka Boris 111

Haiduk, Roman 126–129
Halperin, Alex 36
Hebrew 19, 47, 55, 83, 90, 133, 154
"Hitler," a prisoner 42–43, 67–68
Hitler, Adolf 5, 46–47, 50, 53
Holocaust 54–55
Horbal, Mikola 43, 45
"horse" 17
Horsky, Ella 45
Hrinkiv 149
Hungarians 39

Ilse Koch 38
Inner Mongolia 102
Interior Ministry 118
Iron Curtain 133
Israel 32, 141
Ivan the Terrible 48, 154
Ivanofrankivsk Prison (Kolomyia) 126

Jabotinsky 47
Jerusalem 33, 84
Jews 27, 28, 32, 34, 38, 53–58, 68, 81, 83, 96–97, 103, 110–111, 113, 120, 140, 143, 149, 152, 154
Judaism 47, 55

Kant 114
Karaganda 54, 117
Kazan 134, 136, 152
Kennedy 133
KGB 8–9, 34–35, 40–46, 49–51, 58–59, 70, 76–77, 83, 84, 98, 100, 106, 108, 112–113, 120, 125–128, 130, 132–133, 137, 142, 146, 152, 142, 144, 146, 148–149, 152
Kharkov 62, 125, 153–154
Khazars 54, 65
Khrushchev 56
Kiev 45, 54, 81, 125
Kirov (Vyatka) 87–88, 144
Kiselyov 73, 74, 111, 143
Kizhner, Harry 33
Kolyma 54, 117
Konikov 9
Konstantinovsky, Vladimir 126
Korean plane 133
Korean War 85
Kotov 72, 82, 92
Kotova, Dr. 75
Kovalyov 149
Kovrov 144
Krasniyak 71, 75–76, 131
Kremlin 71–72
Kuban 144
Kudirka, Simas 77, 78, 84, 113

Latvia 40, 51, 122
Lazarev 113
League of Nations 122
Lenin 56, 71, 77, 86
Leningrad 111, 145
Letts 49, 122
Libya 132
Literaturnaya Gazeta [a literary magazine] 57
Lithuania 46–47
Lithuanians 44, 77, 122
Lukyanenko 139
Lyubarsky Kronid 142
Lyubavich 47

Mahnutin 73, 83, 130
Malishev 20–22
Malishko 81
Manchuria 102
Mao Zedong 56
Marchenko Anatoly 37
Markelov 9
Marx 56
Mendelevich Joseph 68, 77–78, 81, 149–150
Mengele 96, 131
Merkushev, Slava 25, 27–29, 32, 98–104
Meshner, Joseph 110
Moldovia 63, 65
Mordovia 25, 70, 78, 104, 109, 112
Moroz, Valentine 130, 139, 148

Index

Moscow 54, 55, 59, 60, 106, 112, 113, 139, 141, 154

Narkhov 25–26
Navasardian, Ashot 146, 148–149, 153
Nazi 33, 35, 49, 61–62, 96, 132
Nixon, Richard 56, 60
NKVD 40

Obrubov 106
Odessa 79
Oedipus 66
Ogurtsov, Igor 105–106, 131–132
Opanasenko 110
Orlovitch 65–66
Orwell 154
Ostrayekov 52

Pasternak 144
the Pechora 65
Penson, Boris 33
Perm 53, 86, 153
Petrov 75, 130, 149
Platonov 77
Plusch 104
Poeta 145
Poland 39, 54, 59, 85
Poles 46
Polish Army (divisions) 59
Poltergeist 19–29
Prihodko, Grigory 129
"The Protocols of the Elders of Zion" 58
"pruning the buds" 45
Pukinskas, Piatras 44
Purim 55, 81, 143

Qumran scrolls 97

Raja Yoga 102
Rakhman 133–137
Red Army 95
Red terror 77
Reznikov, Olexa 78
Rode, Gunar 109, 120, 122–123
Rogov, Valentine 104, 130, 137–139
Rosokhatch 151
Rotenko 73, 83, 130
Russia 19, 39, 47, 50, 52, 56, 58, 60, 67–68, 121, 123, 133, 151
Russo-Japanese War 40
Ryazan 5, 7

Safronov, Alex 84
Sahatian, Roozevelt 146

Samizdat 79
Sapelyak, Stepan 110, 150–152
Semenyuk 98
Sergeyenko, Oles 79–80, 84, 125
Sharikov 83
Shepshelovitch 51
Shimon 68–69
Siberia 55, 81, 95, 117, 133
Simchitch 65
Slobodiyan, Michailo 150
Smolensk 122
solitary confinement 10–11, 14, 25–26, 35, 37, 86, 89, 93, 118, 120, 150
South Africa 133
Soviet Army 25, 140
Soviet health system 131
Soviet navy 140
Soviet Red Cross 131
Soviet Union (empire) 27, 47, 51, 55, 58, 60, 71, 77, 86–87, 89, 96, 101, 104, 116–117, 139
Stalin 5, 46–47, 50, 53, 56, 75, 81, 145
Stalinism 144–145
Stogov, Kostya 144
Stolypin car 87, 89, 146
Suchareva, Larisa 93, 120
Sukharyov 115
Suslensky, Jacob 124
Suslov 144
Sverstiyuk 149
Swiss Committee for Human Rights 142
Syria 140

Tambov 79
Taratokhin, Sergey 148–150
Tataria 134
Technical University for Electronic Engineering 7
Ternopil 151
Tibet 102
Titov 149
Torosian, Sasco 67–68
tortures 44, 77, 81
Trepov 106
Turkey 27

Ugodin 139–140, 142–143
Ukrainians 5, 7–8, 25, 34, 41, 43–45, 49, 51, 53–56, 67, 68, 77, 79, 81, 95, 98, 104, 110, 118, 125–126, 139, 150–154
the United States 60–61, 96, 99, 101, 119
the Ural Mountains 67

157

the Urals 53, 60, 63. 68, 78, 95, 112, 129, 146, 148
Uzbeks 91

Vagin 58
Vandakurov 27, 50–51, 101–103
Vasyukov 115–116
Veduta, Bogdan 35, 96, 104–105
Vladimir Prison 35, 38, 73, 83–84, 87, 89–90, 93, 98–99, 111–113, 118, 129–130, 138–139, 143–144, 152
Vladimirov 116
the Volga 65
Vorkuta 54, 117
Vyetnam 60, 85, 140
Vyetnamese 85

Wallenberg 133
Watergate 60
West 59, 60, 85, 96, 119, 150, 154
West Germany 25

Wissotsky 27
World War II 35, 49, 60, 81, 85

Xinjiang 102

Yatsishin 112, 138
Yerevan 67, 146, 153
Yesenin, Sergey 38
Yiddish 8, 68
the Yom Kippur War 97, 140
Young Guard 55
Yu Xi Lin 108
Yugoslavia 50

Zalmanson, Silva 109
Zalmanson, Zeev 149
Zanosov 21–22
Zdorovy, Anatoly 125–126, 132
Zionists 47, 53–54
Zvegorodny 61, 62

www.ingramcontent.com/pod-product-compliance
Ingram Content Group UK Ltd.
Pitfield, Milton Keynes, MK11 3LW, UK
UKHW042016140426
5217IPUK00015B/1211